LORI BUHLER

Fuss-Free
Machine
Appliqué

Sew on the Line for Great Results

Martingale®
& COMPANY

DEDICATION

To my family: David, my husband, and the love of my life; Amanda, my daughter who gave me Brody, who in turn has a lifetime of Granny's quilts to look forward to.

Fuss-Free Machine Appliqué:
Sew on the Line for Great Results
© 2011 by Lori Buhler

That Patchwork Place® is an imprint
of Martingale & Company®.

Martingale & Company
19021 120th Ave. NE, Suite 102
Bothell, WA 98011-9511 USA
www.martingale-pub.com

CREDITS

President & CEO: Tom Wierzbicki
Editor in Chief: Mary V. Green
Managing Editor: Karen Costello Soltys
Technical Editor: Nancy Mahoney
Copy Editor: Marcy Heffernan
Design Director: Stan Green
Production Manager: Regina Girard
Illustrator: Laurel Strand
Cover & Text Designer: Regina Girard
Photographer: Brent Kane

MISSION STATEMENT

Dedicated to providing quality products
and service to inspire creativity.

Printed in China
16 15 14 13 12 11   8 7 6 5 4 3 2 1

**Library of Congress Cataloging-in-Publication Data
is available upon request.**

ISBN: 978-1-60468-067-6

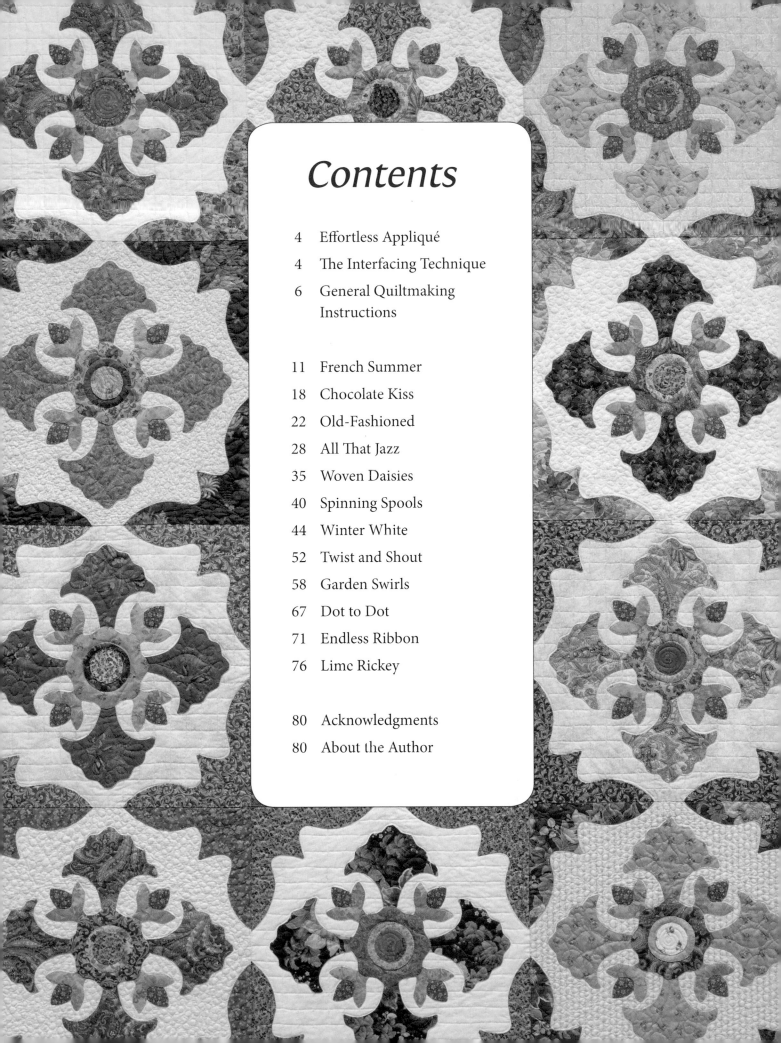

Contents

Effortless Appliqué

I've always admired beautiful appliqué quilts, but was always a little overwhelmed by the thought of all the work that went into making them. When I was introduced to a new interfacing method of appliqué, I knew with this technique I could enjoy the process and not get bogged down by all the fuss that can go into making appliqué quilts. So, with a lot less effort, I could make beautiful quilts to share.

I've made a number of quilts for family and friends over the years, and I always tell the recipients that I would much rather see them use and enjoy the quilt than store it away in order to keep it for "good." A few years ago, our family took a trip to Europe. Family members were coming from different parts of the country and meeting in London. After we had all gathered, we took a shuttle from the airport to our hotel. My niece was a 20-something career girl at the time. As I watched her pull a quilt I'd made for her when she was 10 or 12 from her carry-on bag to cuddle with on the air-conditioned shuttle, I had a couple of conflicting feelings. First, I was amazed that she had carried that quilt with her halfway around the world, and second, I wished that I had made her a nicer quilt if she was going to let the world see it! But I was still happy to see that she was enjoying her quilt after all these years.

Quilts are often used to mark the happy occasions in our lives, and some of the quilts in this book are mementos of those turning points in my family's life: a quilt for my daughter's new apartment, her wedding quilt, and a quilt for my first grandson. I hope you'll find inspiration in these pages to make quilts for some special moments in your life.

The quilts in this book are a combination of appliqué quilts and pieced quilts that use appliqué pieces to emulate the look of curved piecing. This technique used for appliqué is a fast and easy method that fits in with our busy lives. The technique involves using interfacing to face appliqué shapes, making it possible to turn under the edges of the appliqué shapes with perfect results. Some steps of the technique are very portable to take with us to keep our hands busy as we sit at the kids' soccer game, or at the dentist office, or in the car on family vacations.

Some of you may already be familiar with the interfacing technique, but for those of you who aren't or need a brief refresher, I've given step-by-step instructions. The other techniques I've used throughout the book are covered in "General Quiltmaking Instructions" starting on page 6. The remainder of the book is devoted to the 12 projects I designed using the interfacing technique.

This is a great, fuss-free way to do appliqué, and I know you'll love it as much as I do!

- Lori

The Interfacing Technique

Any lightweight non-fusible interfacing can be used for this technique. However, I use a product called Pattern-Ease from Handler Textile Corp., which is similar to interfacing but is classified by the manufacturer as a pattern-tracing material. Like interfacing, it's lightweight and non-fusible, but what I really like about it is that it's 45" wide; most interfacings are only about 22" wide. All the yardage amounts and cutting instructions in this book are based on using a 45"-wide product. If you're unable to find Pattern-Ease or a 45"-wide interfacing, you'll need to double the amount of interfacing yardage required for each project.

1. Follow the project instructions to cut the interfacing into strips the width specified. Then cut fabric strips of the same width.

2. Using a pen, trace the pattern provided with the project onto template plastic. Cut out the template exactly on the drawn lines.

3. Place the template on the interfacing strip and trace around the shape with the pencil. If your template has a straight edge, place that straight edge along the cut edge of the strip. Trace the number of shapes needed, following the illustrations where given to make the best use of your interfacing strip. Leave approximately ½" of space between each shape.

   Note: The interfacing strips are often longer than the fabric strips, so check the lengths against each other to make sure you don't trace more than will fit onto the fabric strip when the strips are layered together.

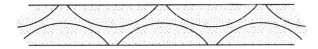

4. Lay the interfacing strip, marked side up, on the right side of the fabric strip of the same width. Be sure that none of the traced shapes are in the selvage area of the fabric strip. Pin the strips together in the areas between the shapes.

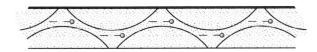

5. Sew on the marked lines, backstitching at the beginning and end of each seam.

6. Cut out each shape, leaving a scant ⅛" to ¼" for the seam allowance. Turn each piece right side out. For shapes that have been completely stitched around, you'll need to cut a slit in the interfacing only, and then turn the shape right side out. I use a turning tool called That Purple Thang from Little Foot Ltd. to help me push out the stitched edges completely. When turning, roll the fabric slightly to the interfacing side to prevent the interfacing from showing on the front of the quilt. Use an iron to press each shape from the interfacing side, making sure

you can see a slight amount of fabric all around the edge.

7. Position the turned shape on the background fabric and machine appliqué it in place along the edges using a blanket stitch or blind hem stitch. You can also use a narrow zigzag stitch, but I don't like it as well, because it tends to flatten the edges of the shape and doesn't look as much like a hand stitch as the blanket stitch or blind hem stitch. This is purely a personal preference. Experiment with the stitches on your sewing machine to find the right stitch for you.

| Blanket stitch | Blind hem stitch | Narrow zigzag stitch |

All my quilts are appliquéd using clear monofilament. You may prefer to use a thread that matches the appliqué piece or even a contrasting thread. I find that using an open-toe foot is helpful for seeing as you sew. Although I machine appliqué my pieces, the interfacing technique may also be used for hand appliqué or the appliqué method of your choice.

8. If the appliqué piece will be part of a seam, such as on the edge of a block, I trim away the fabric and interfacing under the appliqué leaving approximately a ¼" seam allowance. If the piece is not in a seam, trimming is a personal choice. It's not necessary if you'll be machine quilting, but if you're quilting by hand, you may want to cut out the extra layers to reduce the bulk you'll be quilting through.

General Quiltmaking Instructions

In this section you'll find instructions for specific techniques, including making triangle-square units and cutting bias strips, as well as information on the process I use for adding borders. The basics of finishing your quilts are also given here. If you're new to quilting, check with your local quilt shop for beginning quiltmaking classes, or invest in a good reference book, such as *Your First Quilt Book (or it should be!)* by Carol Doak (Martingale & Company, 1997).

BEFORE YOU BEGIN

Here are some points to keep in mind as you sew your projects.

- All yardages listed are based on 42"-wide fabric.

- A rotary cutter, mat, and clear acrylic ruler are needed for rotary cutting. A good pair of sharp scissors is required for cutting out appliqué shapes and trimming away excess fabric.

- Read all instructions thoroughly before beginning any project.

- Prewashing and pressing your fabrics is a personal choice. I rarely prewash my fabrics, but that is my own preference. When in doubt, prewash.

- Sew with the right sides of the fabric pieces together and use ¼"-wide seam allowances unless otherwise specified. Seam allowances are included in the cutting sizes listed, and an accurate ¼" seam allowance is very important for ensuring that the pieces fit together properly.

MAKING TRIANGLE SQUARES

A couple of quilts in this book call for a large number of half-square-triangle units or triangle squares, as I like to call them. The traditional way to make triangle squares is to cut strips ⅞" larger than the finished size of the units. Crosscut the strips into squares, and then cut each square in half diagonally, from corner to corner, to give you two triangles per square. Sew two triangles of contrasting colors together along their long edges to make a triangle square.

Of course there are also many shortcut techniques that you can use to make triangle squares. My favorite is to use Thangles triangle papers. With Thangles, you cut strips ½" larger than the finished size of the unit, layer two contrasting strips right sides together, and then pin the Thangles paper on top. Stitch on the lines indicated on the paper, and then cut on the marked cutting lines using a rotary cutter and ruler. Press the seam allowances toward the darker fabric and remove the paper. When finished, you'll have a number of perfect triangle squares. Thangles papers are available in the sizes needed for the projects in this book.

Another option is to start with two contrasting squares ⅞" larger than your finished triangle square, mark a diagonal line from corner to corner on the wrong side of the lighter square with a pencil, and then sew ¼" on each side of the marked line. Cut the squares apart on the marked line. This will give you two triangle squares.

CUTTING BIAS STRIPS

Bias strips are needed for vine appliqués in several of the patterns.

1. Use a long acrylic ruler and your rotary cutter to square up the left edge of the fabric. Working with a single layer of fabric, place the 45° angle of your ruler along the lower left edge of the fabric. Position the ruler so that it extends completely across the fabric. Cut along the edge of the ruler.

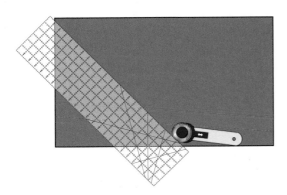

2. Measuring from the cut edge, cut strips the width specified in the project instructions. You're cutting on the bias edge of the fabric, so handle the strips carefully to avoid stretching them.

ADDING BORDERS

All the quilts in this book have borders with butted corners and involve cutting strips from selvage to selvage. These strips may need to be pieced together to achieve the desired length.

1. Place the strips right sides together at a right angle and stitch from corner to corner. Trim the seam allowances to ¼" and press them open.

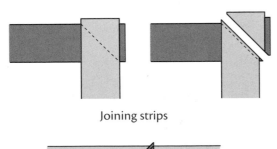

Joining strips

Press seam allowances open.

2. Measure the length of your completed quilt top through the center of the quilt. Cut your side border strips to this measurement. Sew the borders to the sides of the quilt top, easing to fit if necessary. Measure across the width of the top, including the two border strips you just added. Cut the two remaining borders to this measurement and sew them to the top and bottom edges of the quilt. Repeat to add any remaining borders.

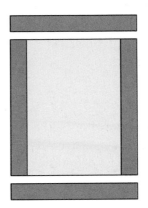

FINISHING TECHNIQUES

Your quilt top may be finished, but there's still a bit more to be done. Follow the guidelines in this section to assemble the quilt sandwich, quilt the layers together, and add the binding and a label.

Layering and Basting

1. Cut the backing and batting at least 1½" to 2" larger on all sides than the quilt top. For most projects, you'll need to piece the backing fabric to achieve the necessary size.

2. Lay the backing wrong side up on the floor or a large, flat surface. Smooth it out and secure the edges with masking tape. The backing should be taut but not stretched. Place the batting over the backing and smooth out any wrinkles. Lay the quilt top, right side up, on top of the batting. Working from the center outward, smooth out the top.

3. Baste the layers together. I use curved safety pins made especially for basting, but you may also thread baste. Place the safety pins no farther apart than a spread hand's width. To thread baste, take long running stitches from the center to each corner, and then create a grid pattern with stitching lines approximately 6" to 8" apart. Baste along the outside edges to finish.

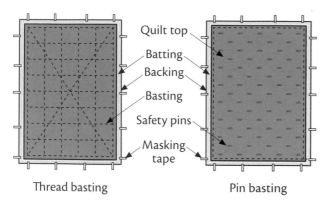

Thread basting   Pin basting

Labels: Quilt top, Batting, Backing, Basting, Safety pins, Masking tape

Machine Quilting

While I am by no means an expert at machine quilting, I have learned a few things over the years. When I first started machine quilting, I mainly quilted in the ditch or followed quilting patterns that I had marked on the top with a stencil. Unfortunately, I often ended up with bumps and puckers. At the time, I was using polyester batting because that was what I had always used for hand quilting. Once I starting using cotton batting, some of these problems were eliminated. Cotton makes the layers stick together and not slide as much.

I've found that marking a quilt top for quilting is one of my least favorite activities, so now I almost always use free-motion quilting that involves no marking. If you've never done this, you really should give it a try. If you can draw it, you can stitch it. You may want to practice on some scrap fabric and batting first.

I use clear monofilament, which doesn't show the inconsistencies in my stitching. I use a regular sewing machine, and although the bed on mine is only a little bit larger than average, it's possible to quilt a large quilt with it. In a quilting class I took a number of years ago, the instructor made a statement that really stuck with me. She said, "As you are pushing the heavy quilt through your machine and

your shoulders are aching, just say over and over, 'It would take me six months to hand quilt this quilt, it would take me six months to hand quilt this quilt. . . .'" So even if machine quilting is sometimes challenging, think how good you'll feel when the quilt is done.

With each quilt's instructions, I include suggestions for the quilting design. I'm usually frustrated by patterns that read "quilt as desired," because I'd like to have at least some idea of how to quilt them. Although I give the details of how I quilted my projects, feel free to quilt yours in any way you please. Maybe my ideas will allow you to think in a different direction for your own quilting.

The following are some general guidelines for machine quilting:

- Basting is important. Make sure all your layers are flat and smooth and that you've used enough pins or thread to prevent the layers from shifting.

- One of the most common forms of straight-line quilting is called "in the ditch." It involves stitching just beside a seam line on the side without the seam allowance. In most cases, this technique requires a walking foot for your machine. A walking foot will help feed all the layers through your machine at the same rate.

- Use an open-toe presser foot and drop the feed dogs for free-motion quilting. This technique allows you to move the quilt in any direction. This is the method I prefer, but it does require practice.

- When you have your quilt in your machine, make sure the area on which you're working is flat and not bunched up. Try to keep the weight of the quilt from pulling at the sewing area, which makes it difficult to move the quilt smoothly as you stitch.

- Free-motion quilting uses a lot of thread, so be prepared. Wind several bobbins before you start so that you don't have to remove the quilt from the machine more often than necessary. Also, make sure you have plenty of thread before you start. It can be very frustrating to be on a quilting roll and then have to stop to make a run to the store for thread.

Binding

I use the overlapped-corners binding method, in which each side of the quilt is bound separately. I also like my binding a bit wider than average, so I use 3"-wide strips rather than the more common 2½"-wide strips. I prefer wider strips because they're easier to sew and I think the binding wears better if it's a little wider. The cutting instructions will indicate the number of 3"-wide straight-of-grain strips to cut.

1. Cut the backing and batting even with the edges of the quilt top.

2. Join the binding strips at right angles to make one long strip. Trim ¼" from the stitching and press the seam allowances open.

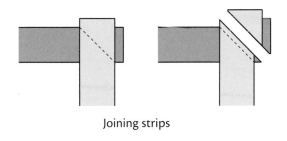

Joining strips

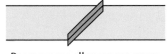

Press seams allowances open.

3. Fold the binding strip in half lengthwise, wrong sides together, and press the entire length.

4. Measure the width of the quilt top and cut two binding strips slightly longer than this measurement. Pin the strips to the top and bottom edges of the quilt front, aligning the raw edges and leaving some excess extending beyond each end. Stitch the binding in place. I use a walking foot and lengthen my stitch length slightly. Trim the ends of the binding strips even with the sides of the quilt.

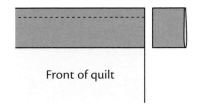

Front of quilt

5. Fold the binding to the back of the quilt and pin it in place.

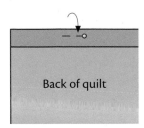

Back of quilt

6. Measure the length of the quilt top and add 2". Cut two binding strips to this measurement. Pin the strips to the sides of the quilt front, aligning raw edges and leaving 1" extending beyond the top and bottom edges. Stitch the binding in place.

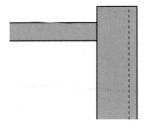

7. On each side, fold the binding up but not over the quilt edge. Fold the excess on each end of the strip over the top and bottom binding, and then fold the remainder of the binding to the back and pin it in place.

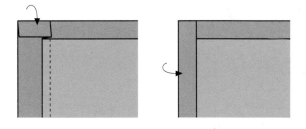

8. Hand stitch the folded edges of the binding in place on the back of the quilt using an appliqué stitch or slip stitch.

Labeling

It's very important that you put a label or some kind of documentation on your quilt. This will help future generations give you proper credit when they're enjoying your skills, or at least make people wonder who you are when they discover your quilt in a dusty corner of an antique shop!

Every label should indicate, at the very least, your name and the date you finished the quilt. I also include the name of the quilt and my city and state. The label can contain as much information as you like. Some things that you might add are the occasion for which the quilt was made and, if it was a gift, to whom it was given. Some quilters have been known to put a few scraps of the fabrics used in the quilt behind the label. These scraps will age at the same rate as the rest of the quilt, so if a repair is needed at a later date, the fabric will be readily available.

You can write your label information directly on the quilt backing with a permanent marker or on a label that you hand appliqué to the backing. The label can be handwritten or computer generated. If you want to use your computer, cut an 8½" x 11" sheet of freezer paper and iron the label fabric to the waxy side. Trim the fabric to the same size as the paper so that you can run it through your inkjet printer. This is a cheap version of photo-transfer paper. I wouldn't recommend this method for anything large or for multiple copies because the printer will sometimes pull the fabric and paper through at an angle, but it will work for a small label.

Another method that I've used for labels is to use the alphabet stitches on my sewing machine. Some of the more basic sewing-machine models don't have this, but many of the newer models have this feature. I fuse interfacing on the back of my label fabric to stabilize the fabric. Follow the instructions for your machine to stitch the letters. I often sew a small border on the label for a decorative touch.

Over the past years, I've made high-school graduation quilts for my nieces and nephews. As part of the backing, I piece their graduation year in large block-style numbers. At the graduation open house, the guests sign their good wishes on the fabric numbers as sort of a guest book. When the young people go off to college, they take not only a warm and cozy quilt, but also the best wishes of their family and friends. I've also included photo-transfer pictures in some of my quilt labels. The photo below shows the label I made for my daughter's wedding quilt, which includes a photo-transfer picture and lettering programmed into my sewing machine.

French Summer

Finished quilt: 72½" x 90½"
Finished block: 18" x 18"

Traditional appliqué blocks take on a new look with appliquéd "photo corners," which form a new pattern where the blocks are joined together.

11

MATERIALS

Yardages are based on 42"-wide fabrics.

This quilt uses a variety of different fabrics for the appliqué pieces. A collection of fat quarters is a good way to get the variety needed. Scraps can be used as well. In my quilt, I used one green fabric for the leaves and one red fabric for the buds.

⅝ yard *each* of 6 assorted beige prints for block backgrounds

4¼ yards *total* of assorted coordinating prints for flower appliqués

2½ yards *total* of assorted dark prints for block corners and border appliqués

2 yards of beige print for outer border

1⅜ yards of red print for inner border and binding

⅜ yard of red print for flower-bud appliqués

⅜ yard of green print for leaf appliqués

5⅜ yards of fabric for backing

77" x 95" piece of batting

4¾ yards of 45"-wide lightweight non-fusible interfacing*

Template plastic

If using 22"-wide interfacing, you'll need 9½ yards.

CUTTING

All measurements include ¼"-wide seam allowances. Cut all strips across the width of the fabric.

From the interfacing, cut:
- 4 strips, 2½" x 45"
- 10 strips, 3½" x 45"
- 7 strips, 6½" x 45"
- 2 strips, 5¾" x 45"
- 6 strips, 10" x 45"

From *each* of the assorted beige prints, cut:
- 2 squares, 18½" x 18½" (12 total)

From the beige print for outer border, cut:
- 8 strips, 7½" x 42"

From the red print for inner border and binding, cut:
- 9 strips, 3" x 42"
- 7 strips, 2½" x 42"

From the red print for flower buds, cut:
- 3 strips, 2½" x 42"

From the green print for leaves, cut:
- 3 strips, 3½" x 42"

MAKING THE APPLIQUÉS

Refer to "The Interfacing Technique" on page 4 for detailed instructions.

1. Make a plastic template of each appliqué shape using the patterns on pages 16 and 17.

2. Using the leaf template, trace 48 leaves onto three of the 3½"-wide interfacing strips, leaving about ½" of space between shapes. *Do not* cut out the shapes.

Leaf arrangement

3. Using the remaining templates, trace the shapes onto the interfacing strips as indicated below, leaving about ½" of space between shapes.
   - Three 2½"-wide interfacing strips: 48 buds
   - Two 5¾"-wide interfacing strips: 12 center flowers
   - Two 3½"-wide interfacing strips: 12 medium flower centers
   - One 2½"-wide interfacing strip: 12 small flower centers
   - Seven 6½"-wide interfacing strips: 48 large flowers
   - Six 10"-wide interfacing strips: 52 block corners

- Five 3½"-wide interfacing strips: 28 border patterns

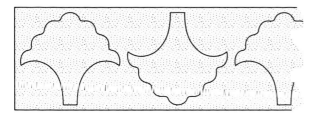

Large flower arrangement

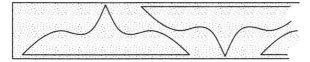

Border pattern arrangement

4. With right sides up, pin the leaf interfacing strips to the green 3½"-wide strips. Sew on the marked lines, leaving the short end of the leaves open. Backstitch at the beginning and end of each seam. Repeat, using the bud interfacing strips and the red 2½"-wide strips.

5. Pin the other interfacing strips to the assorted coordinating fabrics and the assorted dark fabrics for the appliqués. You may have to cut the interfacing strips apart so they fit on the assorted fabric scraps. You'll need four matching corner appliqués and four matching large flowers for each block. Sew on the marked lines of each shape. Edges that go underneath other appliqués or on the outer edge of the block or quilt top can be left open.

6. Cut out the shapes, leaving ⅛" to ¼" for seam allowance. Clip the inner curves. Cut a slit in the interfacing of each shape. Turn the appliqués right side out and use a turning tool to smooth the curves and push out the points. Finger-press the fabric slightly over the interfacing side so that the interfacing won't show on the finished quilt. Use an iron to press each shape from the interfacing side.

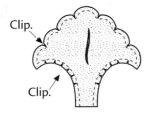

Clip.

Clip.

7. Center a small flower-center appliqué on each medium flower center and appliqué in place using a blanket stitch, blind hem stitch, or narrow zigzag stitch. Then center a flower-center unit on each center-flower and appliqué in place as before.

8. Position each leaf appliqué on top of a bud and appliqué in place in the same manner as before.

APPLIQUÉING THE BLOCKS

1. Pin four matching corner appliqués on each beige square, aligning the straight edges of the appliqués with the corners of the square as shown. Appliqué in place using a blanket stitch, blind hem stitch, or narrow zigzag stitch. You'll have four corner appliqués left over to use for the outer border.

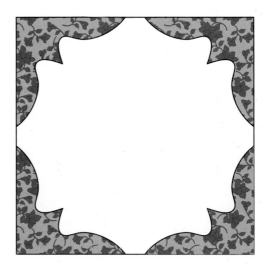

2. Fold each beige square in half and finger-press along the fold. Fold the squares in half in the opposite direction and finger-press the fold again.

3. Repeat step 2 with each center-flower appliqué to mark the centers. Insert a pin through the center of a flower, and then through the center of a beige square. Pin the flower to the square. Repeat for all 12 blocks.

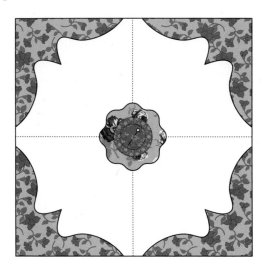

4. Pin the large flowers and the leaves to the beige squares, using the creased lines for placement and tucking the ends underneath the center flower. The large flowers should be approximately 1½" from the edges of the blocks. Appliqué the shapes in place.

5. Trim away the fabric and interfacing behind each corner appliqué, leaving approximately ¼" for seam allowance and being careful not to cut into the top fabric.

ASSEMBLING THE QUILT TOP

1. Lay out the blocks in four rows of three blocks each. Sew the blocks in each row together. Press the seam allowances in opposite directions from row to row. Sew the rows together and press the seam allowances in one direction.

2. Refer to "Adding Borders" on page 7 to measure, cut, and sew the red 2½"-wide strips to the sides, and then the top and bottom edges of the quilt top for the inner border. Repeat to sew the beige 7½"-wide strips to the quilt top for the outer border.

3. Pin the four remaining corner appliqués to the corners of the beige outer border. Pin eight border appliqués on each side of the quilt and six border appliqués to the top and bottom edges of the quilt, spacing the appliqués evenly on each border. Appliqué the shapes in place.

FINISHING THE QUILT

Refer to "Finishing Techniques" on page 7 for detailed instructions.

1. Layer the quilt top, batting, and backing; baste the layers together.

2. Machine quilt in the ditch around each block and along the borders. Free-motion quilt around the appliqué shapes and the flower centers. Quilt a 1" grid of crosshatching in the background of every other block and add stipple quilting in the background of the remaining blocks. In the outer border, quilt a 1½" grid of crosshatching and micro-stipple every other square as shown in the border quilting diagram.

3. Bind the quilt using the red 3"-wide binding strips.

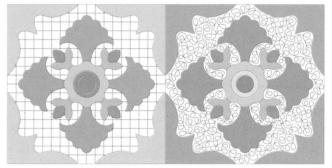

Block quilting diagram

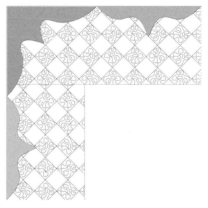

Border quilting diagram

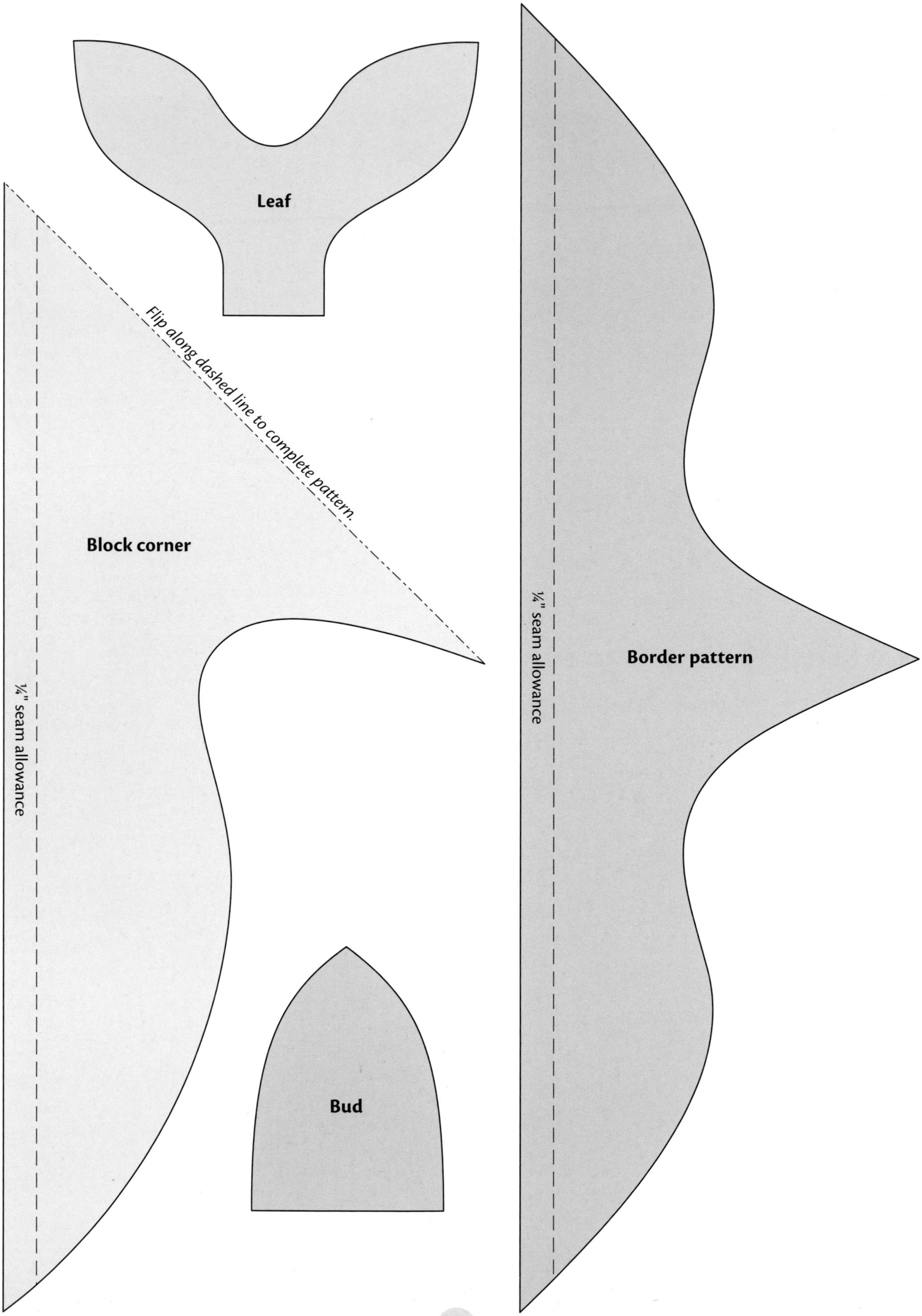

Leaf

Flip along dashed line to complete pattern.

Block corner

¼" seam allowance

Border pattern

¼" seam allowance

Bud

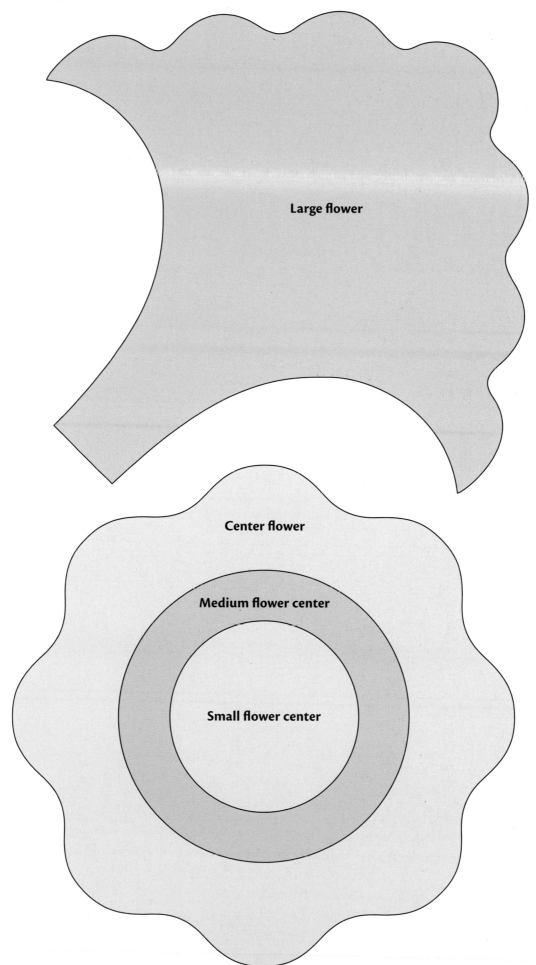

Large flower

Center flower

Medium flower center

Small flower center

Chocolate Kiss

Finished quilt: 64½" x 76½"
Finished block: 12" x 12

This quilt looks like it's made using pieced curves, but the curved shape is actually appliquéd onto half-square-triangle units. What looks like a difficult quilt to make is actually very simple using the interfacing technique.

MATERIALS

All yardages are based on 42"-wide fabric.

½ yard *each* of 10 assorted dark fabrics for blocks

3½ yards of beige print for blocks

2½ yards of multicolored print for outer border and binding

⅝ yard of red print for inner border

4⅝ yards of fabric for backing

69" x 81" piece of batting

2¾ yards of 45"-wide lightweight non-fusible interfacing*

Template plastic

*If using 22"-wide interfacing, you'll need 5½ yards.

CUTTING

All measurements include ¼"-wide seam allowances. Cut all strips across the width of the fabric.

From the beige print, cut:

- 11 strips, 4¾" x 42"
- 9 strips, 6⅞" x 42"; crosscut into 42 squares, 6⅞" x 6⅞". Cut each square in half diagonally to yield 84 triangles.

From *each* of the assorted dark prints, cut:

- 1 strip, 4¾" x 42" (10 total)
- 4 squares, 6⅞" x 6⅞"; cut each square in half diagonally to yield 8 triangles (80 total)

From the interfacing, cut:

- 11 strips, 9" x 45"

From the red print, cut:

- 6 strips, 2½" x 42"

From the multicolored print, cut:

- 6 strips, 6½" x 42"
- 1 strip, 4¾" x 42"
- 6 strips, 3" x 42"
- 2 squares, 6⅞" x 6⅞"; cut each square in half diagonally to yield 4 triangles

MAKING THE BLOCKS

Refer to "The Interfacing Technique" on page 4 for detailed instructions.

1. Sew a beige triangle to a dark triangle to make 80 triangle squares. Press the seam allowances toward the dark fabric.

Make 80.

2. Make a plastic template of the lozenge appliqué shape on page 21. Be sure to trace the center line onto the template.

3. Draw a line through the lengthwise center of each 9"-wide interfacing strip. Using the template and 10 of the interfacing strips, trace eight shapes onto each interfacing strip (80 total), matching the center line on the template with the center line on the interfacing strip. Leave approximately ½" of space between shapes. *Do not* cut out the shapes.

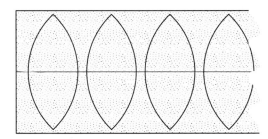

4. Join a beige 4¾"-wide strip to a dark strip along their long edges. Press the seam allowances toward the dark fabric. Make 10.

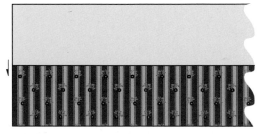

Make 10.

5. With right sides up, pin a marked interfacing strip to each strip set from step 4, matching the center line on the interfacing strip with the seam line. Sew on marked lines, slightly overlapping the stitching at the beginning and end of each seam. Make eight shapes from each strip set.

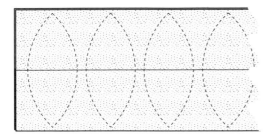

6. Cut out each appliqué shape, leaving approximately ¼" for seam allowance. Cut a slit in the interfacing of each shape and turn the appliqués right side out. Use a turning tool to push out the seams and points. Finger-press the fabric slightly over the interfacing side so that the interfacing won't show on the finished quilt. Use an iron to press each shape from the interfacing side.

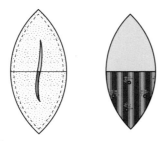

7. Pin appliqué shapes to matching triangle squares, matching the seam lines. The point of the appliqué shape should be approximately ¼" from the corner of the square.

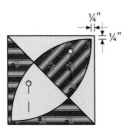

8. Appliqué each shape in place using a blanket stitch, blind hem stitch, or narrow zigzag stitch. Do not trim away the fabric and interfacing behind each appliqué.

9. Arrange four matching appliquéd units as shown. Sew the units together in rows and press the seam allowances in opposite directions. Sew the rows together and press the seam allowances to one side. Make 20 blocks.

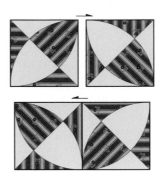
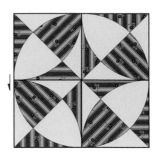

Make 20.

ASSEMBLING THE QUILT TOP

1. Arrange the blocks into five rows of four blocks each. Sew the blocks in each row together. Press the seam allowances in opposite directions from row to row. Sew the rows together. Press the seam allowances in one direction.

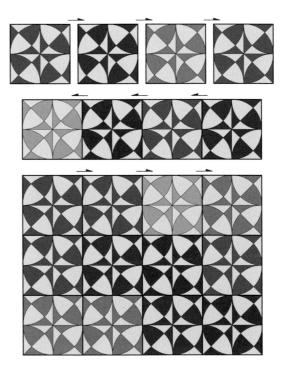

2. Refer to "Adding Borders" on page 7 to measure, cut, and sew the red 2½"-wide strips to the sides and then the top and bottom edges of the quilt top for the inner border.

3. Use the remaining beige triangles and the multicolored triangles to make four triangle

squares. Then use the remaining interfacing strip, beige strip, and multicolored 4¾" strip to make four appliqué shapes as described in steps 3–6 of "Making the Blocks." Pin an appliqué shape to each triangle square, matching the seam lines. Appliqué each shape in place to make four corner blocks.

4. Sew the multicolored 6½"-wide strips together end to end to make a long strip. Measure the width of the quilt top from side to side and cut two strips to this length for the top and bottom borders. Measure the length of the quilt top; cut two strips to this length and sew them to opposite sides of the quilt top. Press the seam allowances toward the border strips.

5. Sew corner blocks to both ends of the top and bottom border strips as shown in the photo on page 18. Press the seam allowances toward the border strips, and then sew the strips to the top and bottom edges of the quilt top. Press the seam allowances toward the border.

FINISHING THE QUILT

Refer to "Finishing Techniques" on page 7 for detailed instructions.

1. Layer the quilt top, batting, and backing; baste the layers together.

2. Machine quilt in the ditch between the blocks and along the borders. Free-motion quilt along the curved edges of the appliqué; then quilt feather and spiral designs in the blocks as shown in the quilting diagram. Quilt a continuous quilting design in the border.

3. Bind the quilt with the multicolored 3"-wide strips.

Quilting diagram

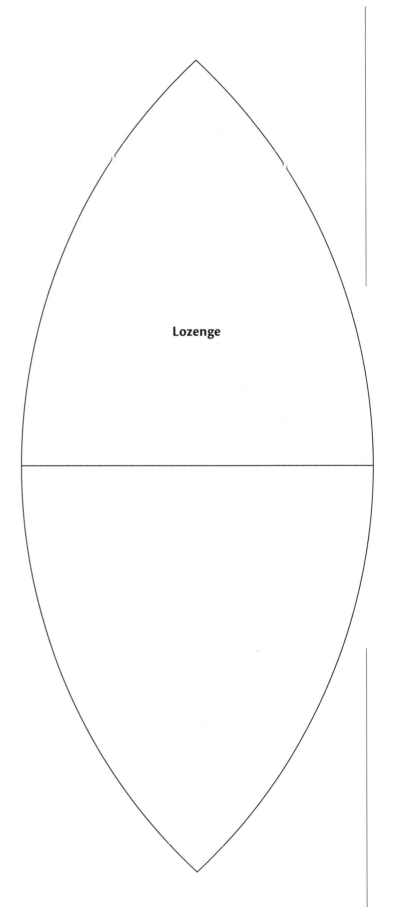

Lozenge

Old-Fashioned

Finished quilt: 72½" x 84½"

Finished block: 6" x 6"

This is an old-fashioned strippy quilt made with a modern technique.
The color palette makes it a happy, cheerful quilt.

MATERIALS

All yardages based on 42"-wide fabric.

2⅜ yards of yellow print for blocks

2¼ yards of white print for appliqué background

2 yards of red print for blocks and binding

1½ yards *total* of assorted coordinating prints for flower appliqués

1½ yards of green print for vine and leaf appliqués

1¼ yards of blue print for blocks

1 yard of polka-dot print for blocks

5 yards of fabric for backing

77" x 89" piece of batting

1¾ yard of 45"-wide lightweight non-fusible interfacing*

Template plastic

Water-soluble marker

*If using 22"-wide interfacing, you'll need 3½ yards.

CUTTING

All measurements include ¼"-wide seam allowances. Cut all strips across the width of the fabric.

From the yellow print, cut:
- 14 strips, 2⅞" x 42"; crosscut into 192 squares, 2⅞" x 2⅞"*
- 23 strips, 1½" x 42"

From the blue print, cut:
- 23 strips, 1½" x 42"

From the red print, cut:
- 14 strips, 2⅞" x 42"; crosscut into 192 squares, 2⅞" x 2⅞"*
- 8 strips, 3" x 42"

From the polka-dot print, cut:
- 12 strips, 2½" x 42"; crosscut into 192 squares, 2½" x 2½"

From the interfacing, cut:
- 2 strips, 4½" x 45"
- 9 strips, 4" x 45"
- 2 strips, 3½" x 45"
- 2 strips, 3" x 45"
- 2 strips, 2½" x 45"

From the green print, cut:
- 4 strips, 4" x 42"

From the *lengthwise* grain of the white print, cut:
- 3 strips, 12½" x 72½"

*Cut 2½"-wide strips, if using Thangles, to make the triangle squares.

MAKING THE BLOCKS

1. Sew one yellow 1½"-wide strip and one blue 1½"-wide strip together along the long edges as shown. Make 23 strip sets. Press the seam allowances toward the blue strip. Crosscut the strip sets into 576 segments, 1½" wide.

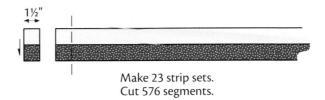

Make 23 strip sets.
Cut 576 segments.

2. Sew two segments together to make a four-patch unit as shown. Make a total of 288 units.

Make 288.

3. Refer to "Making Triangle Squares" on page 6 and use your favorite method to make 384 triangle squares using the red and yellow 2⅞" squares. (If using Thangles, refer to the manufacturer's instructions.) Press the seam allowances toward the red triangles. The triangle squares should measure 2½" x 2½".

Make 384.

4. For each block, lay out three four-patch units, four triangle squares, and two polka-dot squares as shown. Sew the pieces together in rows. Press the seam allowances in the direction indicated by the arrows. Sew the rows together and press the seam allowances toward the center. Make a total of 96 blocks.

 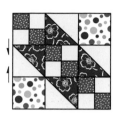

Make 96.

MAKING THE APPLIQUÉ PANELS

Refer to "The Interfacing Technique" on page 4 for detailed instructions.

1. Make a plastic template of each appliqué shape using the patterns on pages 26 and 27.

2. Using the leaf template, trace 79 leaves onto four of the 4"-wide interfacing strips, leaving about ½" of space between shapes. *Do not* cut out the shapes.

3. Using the remaining templates, trace the shapes onto the interfacing strips as indicated below, leaving about ½" of space between shapes.

   - Two 4"-wide interfacing strips: 14 large circle flowers
   - Two 3"-wide interfacing strips: 14 medium circle flowers
   - Two 2½"-wide interfacing strips: 25 flower centers
   - Two 4½"-wide interfacing strips: 11 large tulips
   - One 4"-wide interfacing strip: 11 tulip centers
   - Two 3½"-wide interfacing strips: 18 small tulips
   - Two 4"-wide interfacing strips: 11 roses

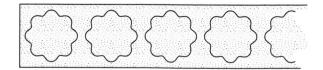

4. With right sides up, pin the leaf interfacing strips to the green 4"-wide strips. Sew on the marked lines, slightly overlapping the stitching at the beginning and end of each seam.

5. Cut the remaining interfacing strips apart as needed to pin the flower shapes to the assorted coordinating prints. Sew on the marked lines, slightly overlapping the stitching at the beginning and end of each seam.

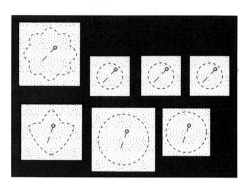

6. Cut out the appliqué shapes, leaving at least ⅛" for seam allowance. Clip the inner points of the flower shapes as needed. Cut a slit in the interfacing of each shape and turn the appliqués right side out. Use a turning tool to smooth the curves and push out the points. Finger-press the fabric slightly over the interfacing side so that the interfacing won't show on the finished quilt. Use an iron to press each shape from the interfacing side.

Clip.   Clip.

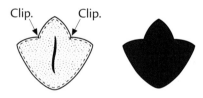

7. Center a flower-center appliqué on each medium circle and appliqué in place using a blanket stitch, blind hem stitch, or narrow zigzag stitch. Then center a medium circle on each large circle and appliqué in place as before. In the same manner, appliqué a tulip center to

each large tulip, and then center and appliqué a flower center to each rose appliqué.

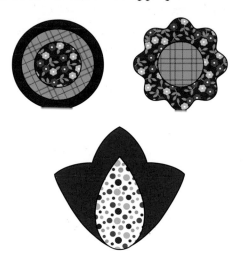

8. Refer to "Cutting Bias Strips" on page 7 to cut 1¼"-wide bias strips from the remainder of the green print for the vines. Piece the strips together and trim them as needed to make three segments, 90" long, and 18 segments, 6" long. Fold each segment in half lengthwise, wrong sides together. Sew ⅛" from the raw edges of each segment. Center the seam under each segment and press it flat. (You may want to use ⅜" bias bars when pressing the vines.)

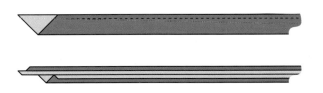

9. With a water-soluble marker, mark the white background strips as follows: Starting at the left edge, measure 6" and make a mark 2" from the bottom. Measure 12" and mark 2" from the top. Continue making marks 12" apart, alternating sides each time. Use a plate to draw a curve at each mark for the vine placement.

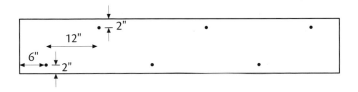

10. With the seam side down, pin the 90" vine segments over the drawn curves. Pin the 6" segments in place, tucking the ends under the long vine as shown.

11. Pin the leaves and flowers to the background panels in a random manner. Refer to the photo on page 22 for placement guidance. Appliqué the flowers, leaves, and vines in place using a blanket stitch, blind hem stitch, or narrow zig-zag stitch.

ASSEMBLING THE QUILT TOP

1. Sew 24 of the blocks together in pairs, and then sew the pairs together as shown to make a block row. Press the seam allowances to one side. Make two of these rows.

Make 2.

2. Sew 12 blocks together to make a side border as shown in the layout diagram on page 26. Press the seam allowances in one direction. Make two side borders. Sew 12 blocks together to make the top border; press. Repeat to make the bottom border.

3. Sew the appliqué panels to the 24-block rows. Press the seam allowances toward the panels.

4. Add the side borders, and then the top and bottom borders. Press the seam allowances toward the appliqué panels.

Quilt layout

FINISHING THE QUILT

Refer to "Finishing Techniques" on page 7 for detailed instructions.

1. Layer the quilt top, batting, and backing; baste the layers together.

2. Machine quilt in the ditch betweem the blocks and along the appliquéd panels. Free-motion quilt around the flowers, leaves, vines, and flower centers; then quilt veins in the leaves. Stipple quilt the background of each panel. Quilt the blocks as shown in the quilting diagram.

3. Bind the quilt using the red 3"-wide binding strips.

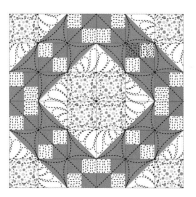

Quilting diagram

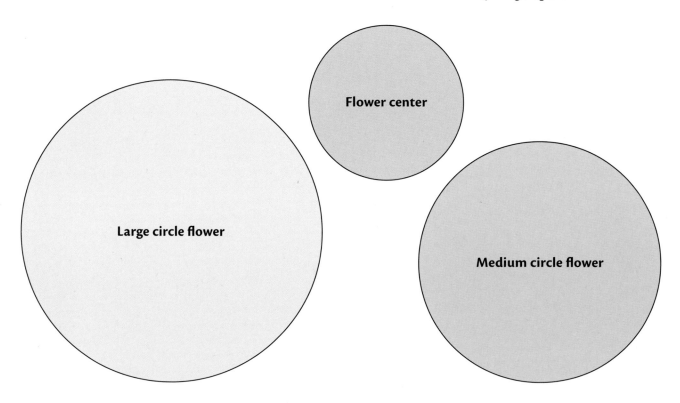

Flower center

Large circle flower

Medium circle flower

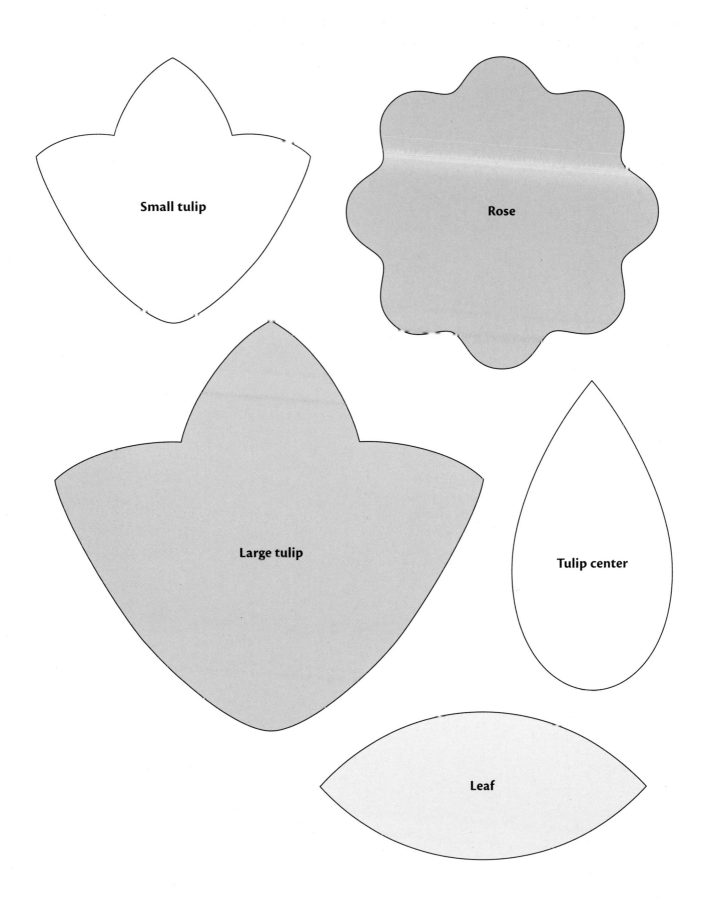

Small tulip

Rose

Large tulip

Tulip center

Leaf

All That Jazz

Finished quilt: 57¼" x 71½"

Finished block: 14¼" x 14¼"

This quilt is "jazzed up" by framing each block with curves that are formed by taking a basic Drunkard's Path block and dividing it up to surround the appliqué block.

MATERIALS

Yardages are based on 42"-wide fabric. Fat quarters measure 18" x 21".

1 fat quarter *each* of 6 assorted dark prints for blocks

1 fat quarter *each* of 6 assorted light to medium prints for blocks

2¼ yards of white-and-brown print for block backgrounds

1⅞ yards of brown print #2 for outer border and binding

1⅛ yards of aqua print for appliqués and inner border

⅞ yard of brown print #1 for appliqués

¼ yard of light print for appliqués

3¾ yards of fabric for backing

62" x 76" piece of batting

2½ yards of 45"-wide lightweight non-fusible interfacing*

Template plastic

*If using 22"-wide interfacing, you'll need 5 yards.

CUTTING

All measurements include ¼"-wide seam allowances. Cut all strips across the width of the fabric.

From the white-and-brown print, cut:

• 3 strips, 8½" x 42"; crosscut into 12 squares, 8½" x 8½"

• 3 strips, 7⅝" x 42"; crosscut into 12 squares, 7⅝" x 7⅝"

• 4 strips, 6" x 42"

From *each* of the assorted dark prints, cut:

• 2 squares, 8½" x 8½" (12 total)

• 1 square, 6" x 6" (6 total)

From *each* of the assorted light to medium prints, cut:

• 2 squares, 8½" x 8½" (12 total)

• 1 square, 6" x 6" (6 total)

From the interfacing, cut:

• 4 strips, 10½" x 45"

• 6 strips, 6" x 45"

• 2 strips, 4" x 45"

From the brown print #1, cut:

• 2 strips, 10½" x 42"

• 1 strip, 4" x 12"

From the aqua print, cut:

• 2 strips, 10½" x 42"

• 6 strips, 2½" x 42"

From the light print, cut:

• 1 strip, 4" x 42"

From the brown print #2, cut:

• 6 strips, 5½" x 42"

• 7 strips, 3" x 42"

MAKING THE BLOCK BACKGROUNDS

Refer to "The Interfacing Technique" on page 4 for detailed instructions.

1. Make a plastic template of the circle pattern on page 33. Use the template to trace 36 circles onto the 6"-wide interfacing strips. Leave approximately ½" of space between shapes. You should be able to fit six circles per strip. Cut apart 12 circles, leaving at least a ¼" space around the circle. Leave the remaining circles joined in strips.

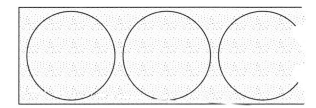

2. With right sides up, pin a marked interfacing strip to each white-and-brown 6"-wide strip. Pin an individual interfacing circle to each light/medium or dark 6" square. Sew on the marked lines, overlapping the stitching at the beginning and end of each seam.

3. Cut out the circles, leaving ⅛" to ¼" for seam allowance. Cut a slit in the interfacing and turn the circles right side out. Smooth out the curves and finger-press the fabric slightly over the interfacing side so that the interfacing won't show on the finished quilt. Use an iron to press each circle from the interfacing side.

4. Using the white-and-brown, light/medium, and dark 8½" squares, fold each square in half and finger-press along the center of the fold. Fold the squares in half in the opposite direction and finger-press the fold again. When you open up the square there should be an X marking the center.

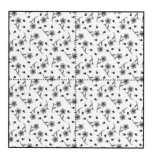

5. Repeat step 4 with each of the white-and-brown, light/medium, and dark circle appliqués to mark the centers.

6. With right sides up, insert a pin through the center of a white-and-brown circle and then through the center of a light/medium or dark square. Rotate the circle so the straight-of-grain of the circle matches the straight-of-grain of the square. Pin the appliqué to the square. Repeat with the remaining white-and-brown circles and the light/medium or dark squares.

7. Repeat step 6, pinning the light/medium or dark circles to the white-and-brown squares.

8. Appliqué the circles to the squares using a blanket stitch, blind hem stitch, or narrow zigzag stitch.

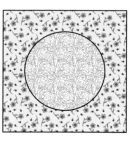 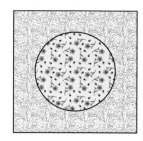

Make 24.   Make 12.

9. Cut each square twice diagonally to make quarter units, keeping pieces with matching fabrics together.

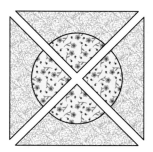

10. On the back of each quarter, trim away the fabric and interfacing under each quartered circle portion, leaving approximately ¼" for seam allowance.

11. Using four matching quarters with white-and-brown backgrounds, sew the pieces to a white-and-brown 7⅝" square as shown. Press the seam allowances toward the outer edges.

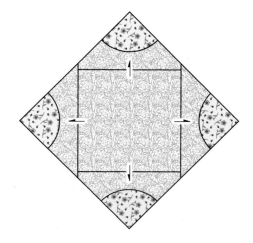

12. Join two matching quarters with light/medium or dark backgrounds as shown to make a corner unit. Make four matching corner units for each block. Sew them to a matching unit from step 11 to complete the block. Press the seam allowances toward the corner units. Make a total of 12 blocks.

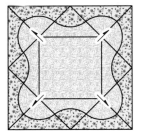
Make 6.

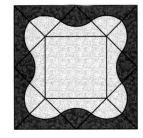
Make 6.

COMPLETING THE BLOCKS

1. Make a plastic template of the large and the small appliqué shapes on pages 33 and 34.

2. Use the large template to trace 12 shapes onto the 10½"-wide interfacing strips. Leave approximately ½" of space between shapes. Use the small template to trace 12 shapes onto the 4"-wide interfacing strips. Leave the large shapes joined in strips and cut the small shapes into two strips of six shapes each.

3. With right sides up, pin two of the interfacing strips marked with the large shapes to the brown #1 print 10½"-wide strips. Pin the two remaining interfacing strips with large shapes to the aqua 10½"-wide strips. Sew on the marked lines, overlapping the stitching at the beginning and end of each seam. Make six brown and six aqua large appliqué shapes.

4. Repeat step 3 using the interfacing strips marked with small shapes, to make six light and six brown #1 print small appliqué shapes.

5. Cut out the appliqué shapes, leaving ⅛" to ¼" for seam allowance. Clip the inner points and curves. Cut a slit in the interfacing of each shape, making the slit as large as necessary, and turn the appliqués right side out. Use a turning tool to smooth out the curves and push out the points. Then finger-press the fabric slightly over the interfacing side so that the interfacing won't show on the finished quilt. Use an iron to press each shape from the interfacing side.

Clip.
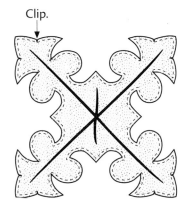

6. Fold the large and small appliqués in half diagonally in both directions to establish center lines. Pin a light small appliqué in the center of each brown large appliqué. Pin a small brown appliqué in the center of each aqua large appliqué. Appliqué the shapes in place, using a blanket stitch, blind hem stitch, or narrow zigzag stitch.

7. Fold each background block in half diagonally in both directions to mark the center. Insert a pin through the center of an appliqué shape and then through the center of a background block. Securely pin the appliqué to the background block. Appliqué the shape in place. Make six blocks with aqua appliqués and six blocks with brown appliqués as shown.

Make 6.

Make 6.

ASSEMBLING THE QUILT TOP

1. Arrange the blocks in four rows of three blocks each, alternating the brown and aqua appliquéd blocks. Sew the blocks in each row together. Press the seam allowances in opposite directions from row to row. Sew the rows together and press the seam allowances in one direction.

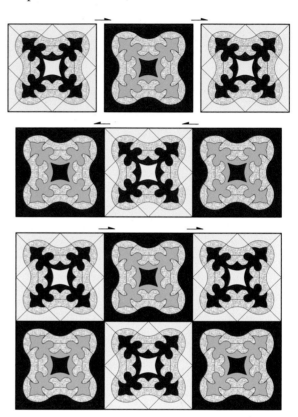

2. Refer to "Adding Borders" on page 7 to measure, cut, and sew the aqua 2½"-wide strips to the sides, and then the top and bottom edges of the quilt top for the inner border. Repeat using the brown #2 print 5½"-wide strips for the outer border.

FINISHING THE QUILT

Refer to "Finishing Techniques" on page 7 for detailed instructions.

1. Layer the quilt top, batting, and backing; baste the layers together.

2. Machine quilt in the ditch between the blocks and along the inner and outer borders. Free-motion quilt around the curved edges and appliquéd shapes in the blocks. Quilt loops in the outer edges and stipple quilt in the background of the blocks as shown in the quilting diagram. Quilt a zigzag design in the inner border and a continuous quilting design in the outer border.

3. Bind the quilt with the brown #2 print 3"-wide strips.

Quilting diagram

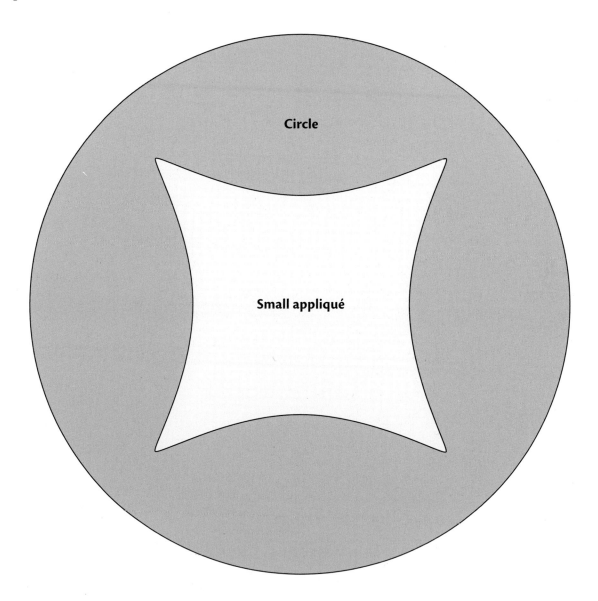

Circle

Small appliqué

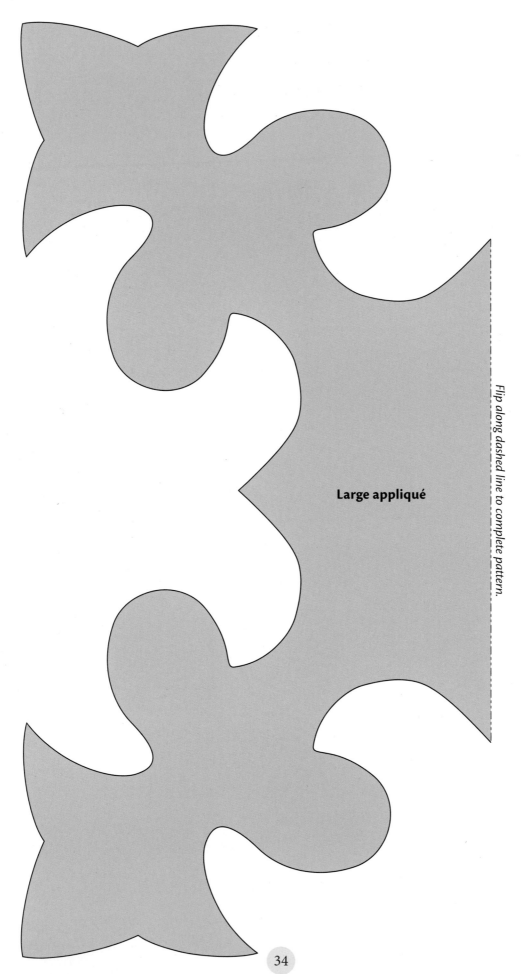

Large appliqué

Flip along dashed line to complete pattern.

Woven Daisies

Finished quilt: 60½" x 72½"

Finished block: 12" x 12"

In shades of the '60s, these friendly daisies float on top
of pieced sashing that appears to be woven.

MATERIALS

Yardages are based on 42"-wide fabrics.

¼ yard *each* of 10 assorted coordinating prints for flower appliqués

3 yards of brown print for blocks, border, and binding

1⅝ yards of light striped fabric for block backgrounds

1⅛ yards of pink print for blocks and border corners

3¾ yards of fabric for backing

65" x 77" piece of batting

1½ yards of 45"-wide lightweight non-fusible interfacing*

Template plastic

Water-soluble marker (optional)

*If you're using 22"-wide interfacing, you'll need 3 yards.

CUTTING

All measurements include ¼"-wide seam allowances. Cut all strips across the width of the fabric.

From the pink print, cut:
- 21 strips, 1½" x 42"
- 1 strip, 3½" x 42"; crosscut into 8 squares, 3½" x 3½"

From the brown print, cut:
- 21 strips, 1½" x 42"
- 6 strips, 6½" x 42"
- 7 strips, 3" x 42"

From the light striped fabric, cut:
- 4 strips, 12½" x 42"; crosscut into 20 rectangles, 6½" x 12½"

From the interfacing, cut:
- 8 strips, 5½" x 45"
- 2 strips, 3" x 45"

MAKING THE BLOCK BACKGROUNDS

1. Sew one brown and two pink 1½"-wide strips together along their long edges as shown. Make seven strip sets. Press the seam allowances toward the brown strips. Crosscut the strip sets into 20 segments, 12½" long. Set aside the remaining strip sets.

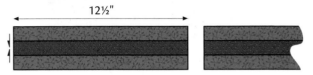

12½"

Make 7 strip sets.
Cut 20 segments.

2. Sew one pink and two brown 1½"-wide strips together along the long edges as shown. Make seven strip sets. Press the seam allowances toward the brown strips. Crosscut the strip sets into 20 segments, 12½" long. Set aside the remaining strip sets.

12½"

Make 7 strip sets.
Cut 20 segments.

3. Sew two pink segments from step 1 to the long sides of a light striped rectangle. Press the seam allowances toward the pink strips. Make 10 blocks.

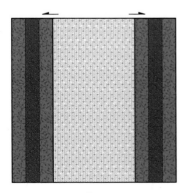

Make 10.

4. Sew two brown segments from step 2 to the long sides of a light striped rectangle. Press the seam allowances toward the brown strips. Make 10 blocks.

Make 10.

MAKING THE APPLIQUÉS

Refer to "The Interfacing Technique" on page 4 for detailed instructions.

1. Make a plastic template of the flower-petal and flower-center patterns on page 39.

2. Use the flower-petal template to trace 20 shapes onto each 5½"-wide interfacing strip (160 total). Leave approximately ½" of space between shapes. Do not cut out the shapes.

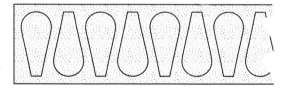

Trace 160 petals.

3. With right sides up, pin 16 interfacing shapes to each of the assorted coordinating prints, cutting apart the interfacing shapes as needed. Sew on the traced lines, backstitching at the beginning and end of each seam and leaving the short ends open.

Leave unsewn.

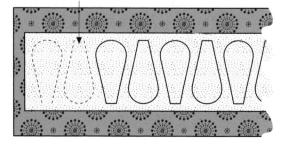

4. Cut out the appliqué shapes, leaving ⅛" to ¼" for seam allowance along the stitched edges and cutting directly on the line at the end of the petal. Cut a slit in the interfacing and turn the appliqués right side out. Use a turning tool to smooth out the curves, and then finger-press the fabric slightly over the interfacing side so that the interfacing won't show on the finished quilt. Use an iron to press each shape from the interfacing side.

5. Use the flower-center template to trace 20 shapes onto the 3"-wide interfacing strips. Repeat steps 3 and 4 to make the flower centers.

COMPLETING THE BLOCKS

1. Fold each block in half and finger-press along the center of the fold. Fold the blocks in half in the opposite direction and finger-press the fold again to establish centering lines. In the same manner create centering lines on each flower center. Place a pin through the center of the flower center, and then through the center of the block background. Pin the flower center in place.

2. Arrange eight matching flower petals evenly around a flower center. You may want to use a water-soluble marker to trace a large circle on the blocks to help space the petals. Pin the petals in place, tucking the ends of the petals under the flower center.

3. Appliqué the flower centers, and then the petals in place using a blanket stitch, blind hem stitch, or narrow zigzag stitch.

ASSEMBLING THE QUILT TOP

1. Arrange the blocks in five rows of four blocks each, alternating the blocks and rotating them as shown to form a woven pattern. Sew the blocks in each row together. Press the seam allowances toward the pink blocks. Sew the rows together and press the seam allowances in one direction.

2. From the remaining pink strip sets, cut eight segments, 1½" wide. From the remaining brown strip sets, cut 16 segments, 1½" wide. Sew two brown segments and one pink segment together to make a nine-patch unit. Press the seam allowances toward the brown segments. Make eight.

Make 8.

3. Sew two nine-patch units and two pink squares together to make a corner block. Make four.

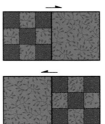
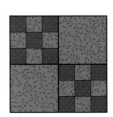

Make 4.

4. Sew the brown 6½"-wide strips together end to end to make a long strip. Measure the width of the quilt top from side to side and cut two strips to this length for the top and bottom borders. Measure the length of the quilt top; cut two strips to this length and sew them to opposite sides of the quilt top. Press the seam allowances toward the border strips.

5. Sew corner blocks to both ends of the top and bottom border strips as shown in the photo on page 35. Press the seam allowances toward the border strips. Sew the strips to the top and bottom edges of the quilt top. Press the seam allowances toward the border.

FINISHING THE QUILT

Refer to "Finishing Techniques" on page 7 for detailed instructions.

1. Layer the quilt top, batting, and backing; baste the layers together.

2. Machine quilt in the ditch around each block. Free-motion quilt around the flower centers and petals; then quilt a spiral in each flower center and echo quilt in each petal. Quilt straight lines in the block background, flower-petal shapes between the blocks, and a continuous quilting design in the outer border.

3. Bind the quilt with the brown 3"-wide strips.

Quilting diagram

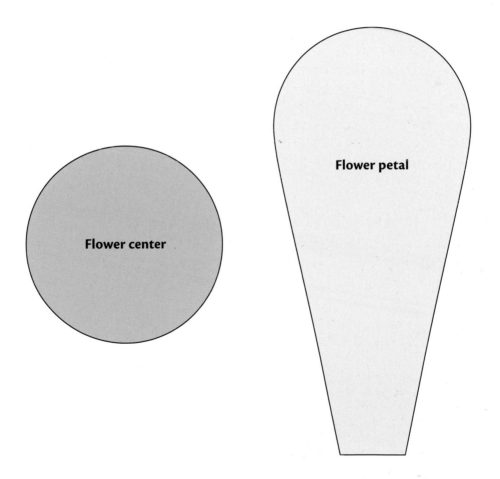

Flower center

Flower petal

Spinning Spools

Finished quilt: 60½" x 60½"

Finished block: 8" x 8"

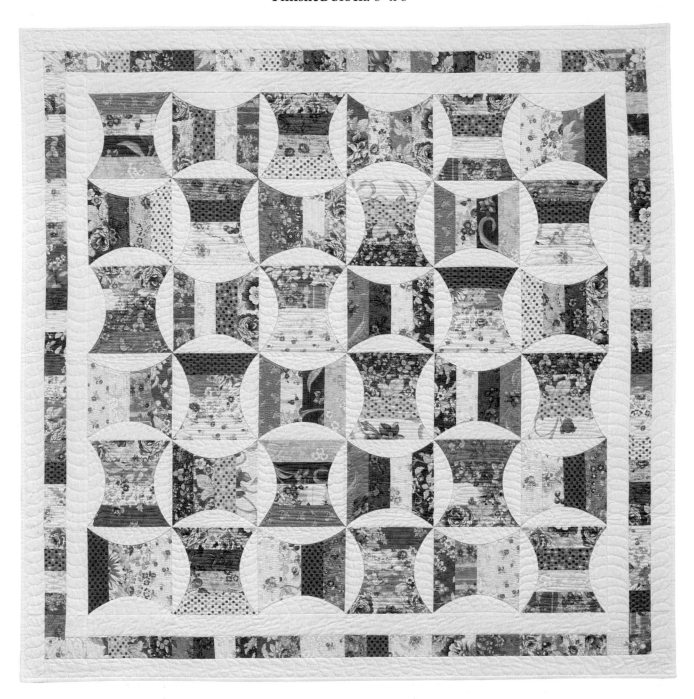

Start with a precut bundle of 2½"-wide strips, sew the
strips into blocks, and then appliqué the white curves
onto the sides to make this spool-like block.

MATERIALS

Yardages are based on 42"-wide fabric.

40 assorted strips, 2½"-wide, for blocks and border

2⅝ yards of white tone-on-tone fabric for appliqués, borders, and binding

3¾ yards of fabric for backing

65" x 65" piece of batting

1 yard of 45"-wide lightweight non-fusible interfacing*

Template plastic

If using 22"-wide interfacing, you'll need 2 yards.

CUTTING

All measurements include ¼"-wide seam allowances. Cut all strips across the width of the fabric.

From the interfacing, cut:

- 9 strips, 3½" x 45"

From the white tone-on-tone fabric, cut:

- 9 strips, 3½" x 42"
- 7 strips, 3" x 42"
- 12 strips, 2½" x 42"; crosscut *2 of the strips* into:

    4 rectangles, 2½" x 6½"

    4 rectangles, 2½" x 4½"

    4 squares, 2½" x 2½"

MAKING THE BLOCKS

1. Join four assorted 2½"-wide strips along their long edges to make a strip set. Press the seam allowances in one direction. Repeat to make a total of 10 strip sets. Cut the strip sets into 8½"-wide segments to make 36 blocks. Set aside the remaining strip sets for the border.

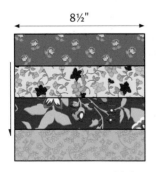
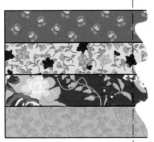

8½"

Make 10 strip sets.
Cut 36 segments.

2. Refer to "The Interfacing Technique" on page 4. Make a plastic template of the arc pattern on page 43.

3. Use the template to trace 72 shapes onto the interfacing strips, aligning the template straight edge with the interfacing long edges and tracing shapes along both sides of the strip as shown. Leave approximately ½" of space between shapes. *Do not* cut out the shapes.

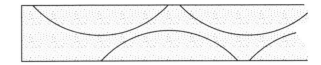

4. With right sides up, pin an interfacing strip to each white tone-on-tone 3½"-wide strip. Sew on the marked lines, backstitching at the beginning and end of each seam.

5. Cut out the appliqued shapes, leaving ⅛" to ¼" for seam allowance. Turn the appliqués right side out. Smooth out the curves and finger-press the fabric slightly over the interfacing side so that the interfacing won't show on the finished quilt. Use an iron to press each shape from the interfacing side.

6. Center and pin an appliqué shape to opposite sides of each block from step 1 as shown, aligning the straight edges. Appliqué the curved edge of each shape in place using a blanket stitch, blind hem stitch, or narrow zigzag stitch. Make a total of 36 blocks.

Make 36.

7. From the wrong side of the block, trim away the fabric and interfacing behind each appliqué, leaving approximately ¼" for seam allowance and being careful not to cut into the top fabric.

ASSEMBLING THE QUILT TOP

1. Arrange the blocks in six rows of six blocks each, rotating every other block as shown. Sew the blocks in each row together. Press the seam allowances away from the white tone-on-tone appliqués. Then sew the rows together and press the seam allowances in one direction.

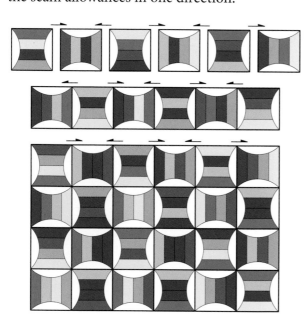

2. From the leftover strip sets, cut 24 segments, 2½" wide. Join six segments end to end to make a 48½"-long border strip. Make four border strips.

Make 4.

3. Using the remaining strip sets, cut three 2½"-wide segments. Separate the segments into four two-square units and four 2½" squares.

4. Using the units and squares from step 3, sew a white tone-on-tone square to an assorted square, and then add a two-square unit. Press the seam allowances toward the darker fabrics. Join a white tone-on-tone 2½" x 4½" rectangle to the two-square unit; press. Sew a white tone-on-tone 2½" x 6½" rectangle to the top of the unit to complete a corner block as shown. Press the seam allowances toward the white rectangles. Make four corner blocks.

Make 4.

5. Join five white tone-on-tone 2½"-wide strips end to end to make a long strip. Make two long strips. From each long strip, cut four 48½"-long border strips (eight total). Sew white border strips to both long sides of each pieced border strip to make four borders. Press the seam allowances toward the white strips.

Make 4.

6. Sew border strips to opposite sides of the quilt top. Press the seam allowances toward the border strips. Sew corner blocks to both ends of the two remaining border strips as shown. Press the seam allowances toward the border strips, and then sew the strips to the top and bottom edges of the quilt top. Press the seam allowances toward the borders.

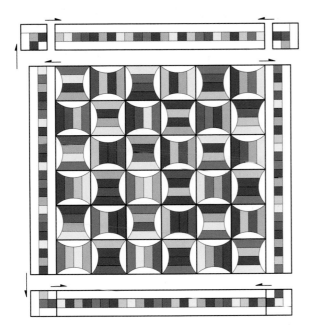

FINISHING THE QUILT

Refer to "Finishing Techniques" on page 7 for detailed instructions.

1. Layer the quilt top, batting, and backing; baste the layers together.

2. Machine quilt in the ditch around each block and along the borders. Free-motion quilt around the block appliqués; then quilt the blocks as shown in the quilting diagram. Quilt a continuous quilting design in the borders.

3. Bind the quilt with the white tone-on-tone 3"-wide strips.

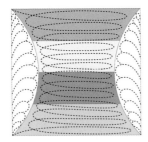

Quilting diagram

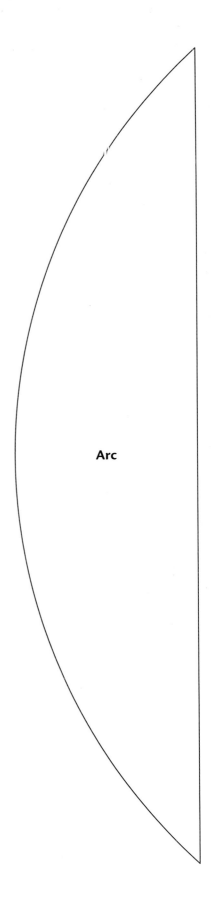

Arc

Winter White

Finished quilt: 76½" x 85"

Subtle, yet elegant, this is my version of a "white-on-white" quilt. The background is a patchwork of beiges and tans that sets off the white appliqué pieces.

MATERIALS

Yardages are based on 42"-wide fabrics.

5¾ yards of off-white tone-on-tone fabric for appliqués, borders, and binding

5 yards *total* of assorted beige and tan prints for quilt center and borders*

5¼ yards of fabric for backing

81" x 90" piece of batting

2¾ yards of 45"-wide lightweight non-fusible interfacing**

Template plastic

Water-soluble marker

Note: The more tan and beige prints you use the better. Great way to use up those scraps!

**If you're using 22"-wide interfacing, you'll need 5½ yards.*

CUTTING

All measurements include ¼"-wide seam allowances. Cut all strips across the width of the fabric.

From the interfacing, cut:
- 2 strips, 15" x 45"
- 1 strip, 12" x 45"
- 3 strips, 9" x 45"
- 3 strips, 7" x 45"
- 1 strip, 3" x 45"

From the off-white tone-on-tone fabric, cut:
- 2 strips, 15" x 42"
- 1 strip, 12" x 42"
- 3 strips, 9" x 42"
- 3 strips, 7" x 42"
- 13 strips, 4¾" x 42"
- 10 strips, 3" x 42"

From the assorted beige and tan prints, cut:
- 355 squares, 3½" x 3½"
- 14 squares, 3" x 3"; cut in half diagonally to yield 28 half-square triangles
- 71 squares, 5½" x 5½"; cut into quarters diagonally to yield 284 quarter-square triangles

MAKING THE APPLIQUÉS

Refer to "The Interfacing Technique" on page 4 for detailed instructions.

1. Make plastic templates for shapes A–F using the patterns on pages 49–51.

2. Using the A template, trace two and two reversed shapes (four total) onto the 12"-wide interfacing strip. Leave approximately ¼" of space between shapes. Do not cut out the shapes.

3. Using the remaining templates, trace the shapes onto the interfacing strips as indicated below in the same manner as before.
   - Two 15"-wide interfacing strips: eight and eight reversed of shape B
   - Three 9"-wide interfacing strips: 34 of shape C
   - One 7"-wide interfacing strip: 12 of shape D
   - Two 7"-wide interfacing strips: 14 and 14 reversed of shape E
   - One 3"-wide interfacing strip: eight of shape F

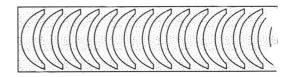

4. With right sides up, pin the interfacing strips to the same-size off-white strips. Sew on the traced lines of each shape, backstitching at the beginning and end of each seam and leaving the short ends of pieces A–E open.

5. Cut out the appliqué shapes, leaving ⅛" to ¼" for seam allowance. Clip the inner curves of each shape. Cut a slit in the interfacing of each shape and turn the appliqués right side out. Cut the slit as long as necessary to make turning easy. Use a turning tool to smooth out the curves and push out the points. Finger-press the fabric slightly over the interfacing side so that the interfacing won't show on the finished quilt. Use an iron to press each shape from the interfacing side. Set the appliqués aside.

PIECING THE QUILT CENTER AND BORDERS

1. Lay out beige squares and triangles in diagonal rows as shown. Join the pieces in each row. Press the seam allowances in opposite directions from row to row. Join the rows and press the seam allowances in one direction.

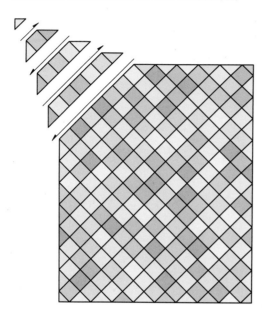

2. On the patchwork center, position two A and two A reversed appliqués, placing them approximately 4½" from the outer edge and pin in place. On each end, pin three D, two E, and two E reversed appliqués; evenly fan out the appliqués. Then pin one F appliqué at the base of the fan covering the open ends of the D and E appliqués. On each side, pin one D, one E, one E reversed, and one F appliqué.

3. Appliqué the shapes in place using a blanket stitch, blind hem stitch, or narrow zigzag stitch.

4. To make the first patchwork border, sew together two beige 3½" squares and two beige quarter-square triangles, as shown. Make 46 of these units.

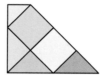

Make 46.

5. Sew together two beige squares, three beige quarter-square triangles, and one beige half-square triangle to make corner unit 1. Join one beige square, two beige quarter-square triangles, and one beige half-square triangle to make corner unit 2. Make four of each corner unit.

Corner unit 1.
Make 4.

Corner unit 2.
Make 4.

6. For each side border, join 11 units from step 4, one corner unit 1, and one corner unit 2 as shown. Make two side borders.

Make 2.

7. For the top border, join 12 units from step 4, one corner unit 1, and one corner unit 2 as shown. Repeat to make the bottom border.

Make 2.

8. To make the outer patchwork border, sew together one beige square and two quarter-square triangles as shown. Make 64 of these units.

Make 64.

9. Use one beige square, one beige quarter-square triangle, and two beige half-square triangles to make eight corner units as shown.

Corner unit 3.
Make 8.

10. Join 16 units from step 8 and two corner units from step 9 as shown to make a border strip. Make four.

Make 4.

ASSEMBLING THE QUILT TOP

1. Referring to "Adding Borders" on page 7 and using six of the off-white 4¾"-wide strips, measure, cut, and sew the inner border to the sides, and then the top and bottom edges of the quilt center. Press the seam allowances toward the off-white strips.

2. Sew the first patchwork border to the sides, and then the top and bottom edges of the quilt top. Press the seam allowances toward the off-white strips.

3. Pin two B and two B reversed appliqués to each border, starting in the center and positioning the second appliqué so that it covers the open end of the first appliqué. On the top and bottom borders, the appliqués will overlap more, and you'll need to trim them to fit the border. In each corner, pin one D, two E, and two E reversed appliqués; evenly fan out the appliqués. Pin F appliqués at the base of the fans, covering the open ends of the D and E appliqués. Appliqué the pieces in place.

4. Use the remaining off-white 4¾"-wide strips to measure, cut, and sew the third border to the sides, and then the top and bottom edges of the quilt center. Press the seam allowances toward the off-white strips.

5. With right sides together, evenly space nine C appliqués along the sides of the off-white border, aligning the straight edges and making sure to leave ¼" seam allowance at each end. Pin in place. Pin eight C appliqués along the top and bottom borders. (You might want to pin the

appliqués at each end out of the way to avoid catching them in the seam line.)

6. Sew an outer patchwork border to the sides, and then the top and bottom edges of the quilt top, covering the appliqués. Press the seam allowances toward the off-white border.

7. Position the appliqués on top of the patchwork border and press. Appliqué the shapes in place.

FINISHING THE QUILT

Refer to "Finishing Techniques" on page 7 for detailed instructions.

1. Layer the quilt top, batting, and backing; baste the layers together.

2. Machine quilt in the ditch between the squares of the quilt center and along the seam line for the borders. Free-motion quilt around the edges of the appliqués. In the patchwork area of the quilt center, use a water-soluble marker to draw lines dividing each square into a four-patch unit. Quilt on the lines, and then micro-stipple in alternating squares. Quilt a scalloped border design in each off-white border. In the first patchwork border, quilt a zigzag pattern in each square, alternating directions from square to square. In the outer patchwork border, echo quilt inside each appliqué, and then quilt loops around the outside of the appliqués.

3. Bind the quilt with the remaining off-white 3"-wide strips.

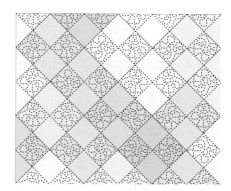

Patchwork-center quilting diagram

Inner-border patchwork quilting diagram

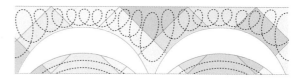

Outer-border patchwork quilting diagram

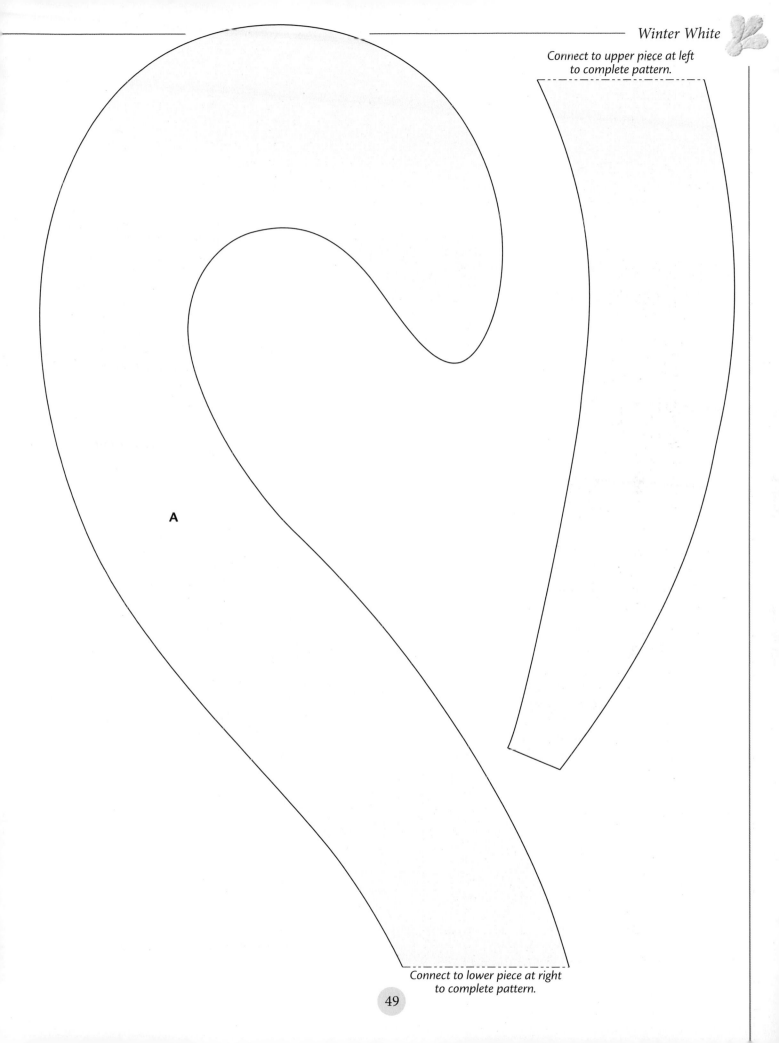

Connect to upper piece at left
to complete pattern.

A

Connect to lower piece at right
to complete pattern.

Connect to upper piece at left
to complete pattern.

B

Connect to lower piece at right
to complete pattern.

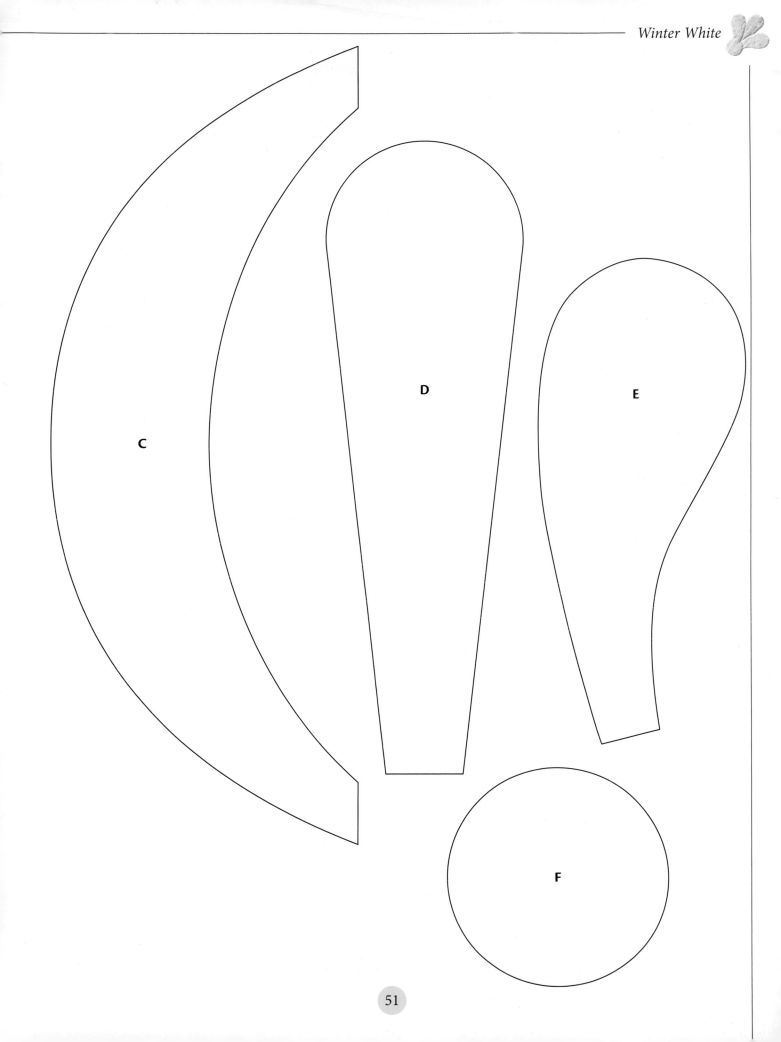

C

D

E

F

Twist and Shout

Finished quilt: 54½" x 54½"
Finished block: 18" x 18"

With swirls that flow around each block, this is a fun quilt
to make using a variety of fabrics. An assortment of
precut 10" fabric squares was used for the appliqués.

MATERIALS

Yardages are based on 42"-wide fabrics.

30 assorted 10" squares for appliqués

2½ yards of light print for block backgrounds and outer border

1¼ yards of red print for sashing, inner border, and binding

3½ yards of fabric for backing

59" x 59" piece of batting

2 yards of 45"-wide lightweight non-fusible interfacing*

Template plastic

If using 22"-wide interfacing, you'll need 4 yards.

CUTTING

All measurements include ¼"-wide seam allowances. Cut all strips across the width of the fabric.

From the interfacing, cut:
- 3 strips, 8" x 45"
- 16 squares, 10" x 10"

From the light print, cut:
- 4 squares, 18½" x 18½"
- 5 strips, 6½" x 42"

From the red print, cut:
- 6 strips, 3" x 42"
- 7 strips, 2½" x 42"; crosscut *2 of the strips* into:
     1 strip, 2½" x 38½"
     2 strips, 2½" x 18½"

APPLIQUÉING THE BLOCKS

Refer to "The Interfacing Technique" on page 4 for detailed instructions.

1. Make a plastic template for shapes A–E using the patterns on pages 55–57.

2. Using templates A–D, trace a variety of shapes onto the 10" interfacing squares. Leave approximately ½" of space between shapes. You'll be able to fit one large shape (shape A or B) and a few of the smaller shapes on each square. Some shapes can extend beyond the edges of the

square. Flip the template over and trace some reversed shapes. Do not cut out the shapes.

3. With right sides up, pin each interfacing square to an assorted 10" square. Sew on the marked lines, leaving the short ends of the shapes open. Backstitch at the beginning and end of each seam.

4. Cut out the appliqué shapes, leaving approximately ¼" for seam allowance. Clip the inner curves of each shape. Cut a slit in the interfacing of each shape and turn the appliqués right side out. Use a turning tool to smooth out the curves and push out the points. Finger-press the fabric slightly over the interfacing side so that the interfacing won't show on the finished quilt. Use an iron to press each shape from the interfacing side.

5. Randomly position appliqués on each light square, tucking the open ends under other appliqués or off the edge of the light square. Refer to the photo on page 52 for placement guidance as needed. Pin the appliqués in place.

6. Appliqué each shape in place using a blanket stitch, blind hem stitch, or narrow zigzag stitch. Do not trim away the fabric and interfacing behind each appliqué. Make four blocks. Square up the blocks.

ASSEMBLING THE QUILT TOP

1. Join two blocks with a red 18½"-long strip to make a block row. Make two of these rows. Sew the two block rows and the red 38½"-long strip together as shown. Press the seam allowances toward the red strips.

2. Refer to "Adding Borders" on page 7 to measure, cut, and sew the remaining red 2½"-wide strips to the sides, and then the top and bottom edges of the quilt top for the inner border. Repeat using the light 6½"-wide strips for the outer border.

3. Using the C and E templates, trace 12 C and 12 C reversed shapes and four E shapes onto the 8"-wide interfacing strips. Cut the strips apart between the shapes, leaving at least a ¼" margin of interfacing.

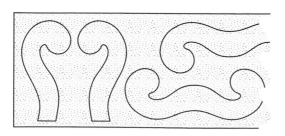

4. With right sides up, pin the shapes to the remaining assorted 10" squares. In the same manner as before, sew on the marked lines and cut out the shapes, leaving a ¼" seam allowance. Turn the appliqués right side out.

5. Pin an E appliqué in the center of each light border. Pin three C appliqués on each side of the E appliqué as shown, tucking the open ends under the previous appliqué. Appliqué the pieces in place.

FINISHING THE QUILT

Refer to "Finishing Techniques" on page 7 for detailed instructions.

1. Layer the quilt top, batting, and backing; baste the layers together.

2. Machine quilt in the ditch around each block and on each side of the sashing and inner border. Free-motion quilt around the edges of the appliqués. Quilt a stipple pattern in the background of the blocks and the outer border. Quilt a continuous design in the sashing and inner border.

3. Bind the quilt with the red 3"-wide strips.

A

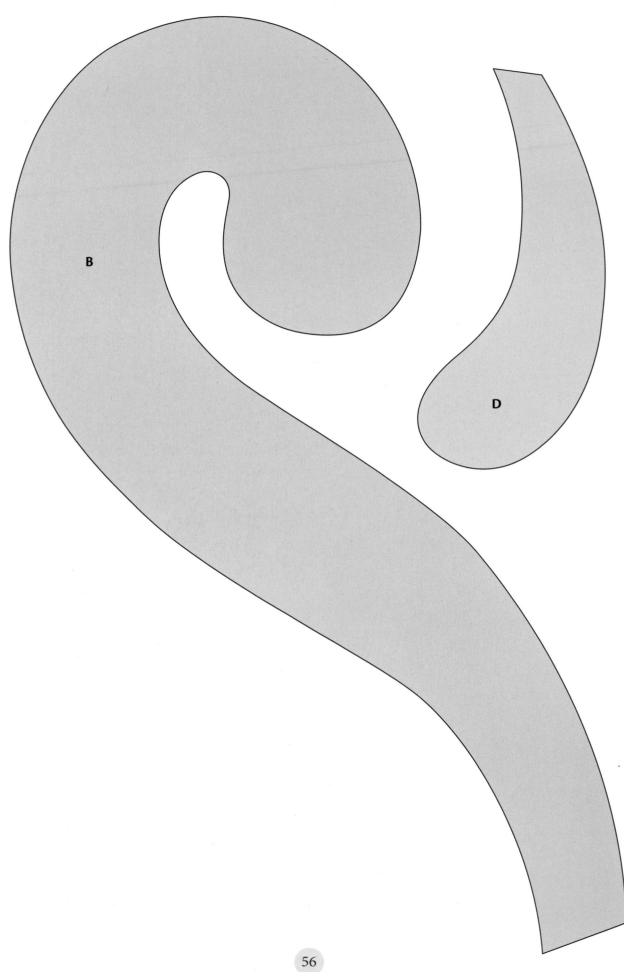

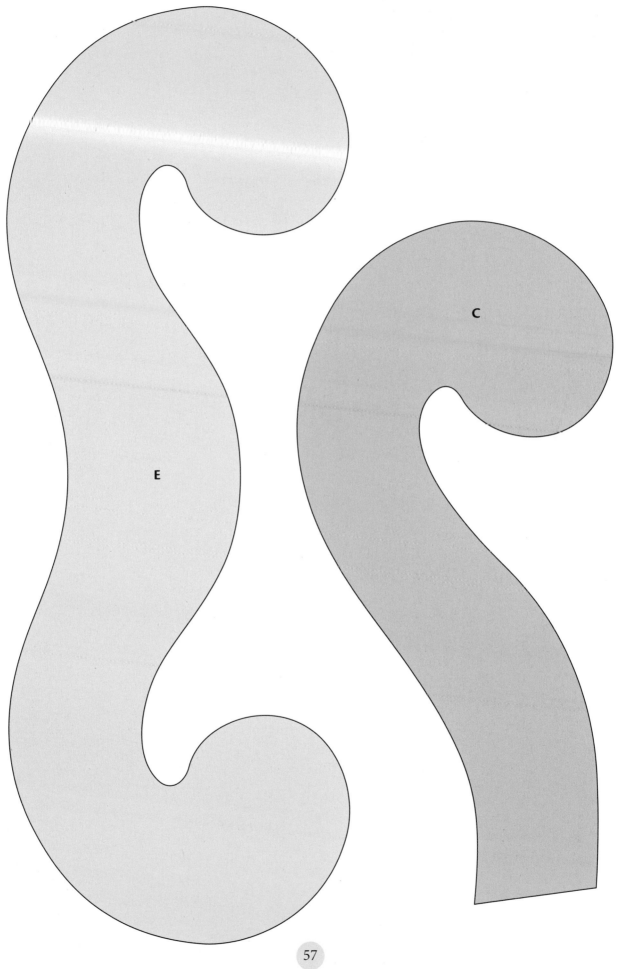

Garden Swirls

Finished quilt: 84½" x 84½"
Finished block: 20" x 20"

"Garden Swirls" is basically a four-block quilt—but with pizzazz!
The appliqué blocks swirling into the border contrast with the
straight-line chains that crisscross the quilt. Truly a stunner!

MATERIALS

Yardages are based of 42"-wide fabrics.

4¾ yards of light print for block backgrounds

4½ yards of multicolored print for borders and binding

2 yards of green print for stem and leaf appliqués

1⅝ yards of dark purple print for blocks and flower appliqués

1⅜ yards of pink print for block appliqués

¾ yard of medium purple print for flower appliqués

⅜ yard of light purple print for flower appliqués

7½ yards of fabric for backing

89" x 89" piece of batting

3 yards of 45"-wide lightweight non-fusible interfacing*

Template plastic

Water-soluble marker

If using 22"-wide interfacing, you'll need 6 yards.

CUTTING

All measurements include ¼"-wide seam allowances. Cut all strips across the width of the fabric.

From the light print, cut:
• 2 strips, 12½" x 42"
• 2 strips, 8½" x 42"
• 7 strips, 4½" x 42"
• 4 squares, 20½" x 20½"

From the dark purple print, cut:
• 11 strips, 4½" x 42"
• 1 strip, 2" x 42"

From the interfacing, cut:
• 3 strips, 7" x 45"
• 5 strips, 6½" x 45"
• 2 strips, 5" x 45"
• 3 strips, 4½" x 45"
• 4 strips, 4" x 45"
• 2 strips, 3¾" x 45"
• 2 strips, 2½" x 45"
• 1 strip, 2" x 45"

From the pink print, cut:
• 5 strips, 6½" x 42"
• 2 strips, 4½" x 42"

From the multicolored print, cut:
• 2 strips, 20½" x 42"; crosscut into 4 rectangles, 12½" x 20½"
• 4 strips, 12½" x 42"; crosscut into 4 rectangles, 12½" x 32½"
• 1 strip, 8½" x 42"
• 1 strip, 4½" x 42"
• 2 strips, 3¾" x 42"
• 9 strips, 3" x 42"
• 1 strip, 2½" x 42"

From the green print, cut:
• 4 strips, 4" x 42"
• 1 strip, 4½" x 42"
• 1 strip, 2½" x 42"

From the medium purple print, cut:
• 3 strips, 7" x 42"

From the light purple print:
• 2 strips, 5" x 42"

MAKING THE CHAIN BLOCKS

1. Sew two dark purple 4½"-wide strips and one light 12½"-wide strip together along their long edges as shown to make strip set A. Make two strip sets. Press the seam allowances toward the purple strips. Crosscut the strip sets into 10 segments, 4½" wide. Set aside the remaining strip set.

Strip set A.
Make 2. Cut 10 segments.

2. Sew two dark purple 4½"-wide and three light 4½"-wide strips together along their long edges as shown to make strip set B. Make two strip sets. Press the seam allowances toward the purple strips. Crosscut the strip sets into 10 segments, 4½" wide.

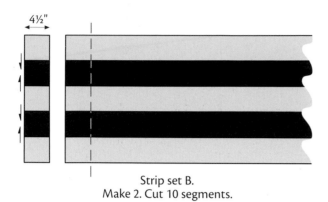

4½"

Strip set B.
Make 2. Cut 10 segments.

3. Sew one dark purple 4½"-wide and two light 8½"-wide strips together along the long edges as shown to make strip set C. Press the seam allowances toward the purple strip. Crosscut the strip set into five segments, 4½" wide.

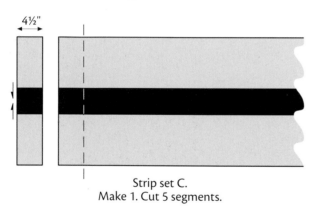

4½"

Strip set C.
Make 1. Cut 5 segments.

4. Join two A segments, two B segments, and one C segment as shown to make a block. Make five Chain blocks.

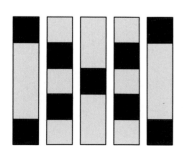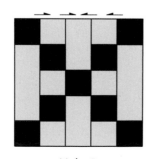

Make 5.

5. Refer to "The Interfacing Technique" on page 4 for detailed instructions. Make a plastic template of patterns A and B on page 65. Using template A, trace 56 shapes onto the 6½"-wide interfacing strips. Leave approximately ½" of space between shapes. Do not cut out the shapes.

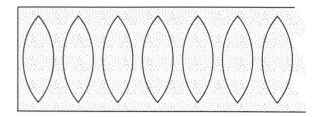

6. With right sides up, pin a marked interfacing strip to each pink 6½"-wide strip. Sew on the marked lines, slightly overlapping the stitching at the beginning and end of each seam.

7. Cut out the shapes, leaving ⅛" to ¼" for seam allowance. Cut a slit in the interfacing of each shape and turn the appliqués right side out. Use a turning tool to smooth the curves and push out the points. Finger-press the fabric slightly over the interfacing side so that the interfacing won't show on the finished quilt. Use an iron to press each shape from the interfacing side.

8. Use template B to trace nine shapes onto two 4½"-wide interfacing strips. Using the pink 4½"-wide strips, repeat steps 6 and 7 to make nine B shapes.

9. Make a plastic template of the circle pattern on page 65. In the same manner as before and using the multicolored 2½"-wide strip and one 2½"-wide interfacing strip, make nine circle appliqués for the block centers.

10. Place a circle in the center of each pink B appliqué as shown. Appliqué in place using a blind hem stitch, buttonhole stitch, or narrow zigzag stitch. Make nine appliquéd B units.

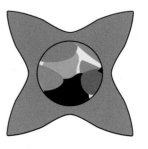

11. Pin an appliquéd B unit to the center square of a Chain block as shown. Pin pink A appliqués diagonally on each remaining dark purple square. Appliqué the pieces in place. Set aside the remaining pieces to be used for the border units.

PIECING THE BORDER UNITS

1. Sew the multicolored 8½"-wide strip and a dark purple 4½"-wide strip together as shown. Press the seam allowances toward the purple strip. Crosscut the strip set into eight 4½"-wide segments.

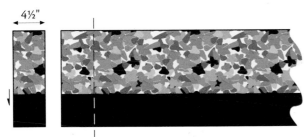

4½"

Make 1 strip set.
Cut 8 segments.

2. Sew the multicolored 4½"-wide strip, the remaining dark purple 4½"-wide strip, and the remaining light 4½"-wide strip together as shown. Press the seam allowances toward the purple strip. Crosscut the strip set into eight 4½"-wide segments.

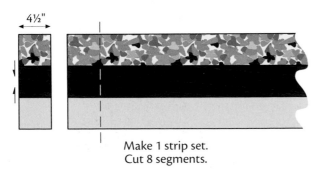

4½"

Make 1 strip set.
Cut 8 segments.

3. From the remaining A strip set, cut four 4½"-wide segments. Remove one dark purple square from each segment; then trim the light rectangle so that each segment measures 4½" x 12½".

Make 4.

4. Sew the units from steps 1–3 together as shown to make four border units.

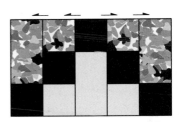

Make 4.

5. Pin four pink A appliqués and one appliquéd B unit to each border unit as shown. Appliqué the pieces in place.

MAKING THE APPLIQUÉS

Refer to "The Interfacing Technique" on page 4 for detailed instructions.

1. Make plastic templates of the leaf, rose, large flower, medium flower, flower base, and flower center patterns on pages 65 and 66.

2. Use the templates to trace the shapes onto the interfacing strips as indicated below. Leave approximately ½" of space between shapes. Do not cut out the shapes.

   - Four 4"-wide interfacing strips: 64 leaves
   - Two 3¾"-wide interfacing strips: 16 roses
   - One 2"-wide interfacing strip: 16 flower centers
   - Three 7"-wide interfacing strips: 16 large flowers
   - Two 5"-wide interfacing strip: 16 medium flowers
   - One 2½"-wide interfacing strip: 16 flower bases
   - One 4½"-wide interfacing strip: four of shape B

3. With right sides up, pin the interfacing strips to the fabric strips as indicated.

   - Leaf interfacing strips to green 4"-wide strips
   - Flower-base interfacing strip to green 2½"-wide strip
   - Shape-B interfacing strip to green 4½"-wide strip
   - Rose interfacing strips to multicolored 3¾"-wide strips
   - Flower-center interfacing strips to dark purple 2"-wide strip
   - Large-flower interfacing strips to medium purple 7"-wide strips
   - Medium-flower interfacing strip to light purple 5"-wide strip

   Sew on the marked lines, slightly overlapping the stitching at the beginning and end of each seam.

4. Cut out the appliqué shapes, leaving ⅛" to ¼" for seam allowance. Clip the inner points of the shapes. Cut a slit in the interfacing of each shape and turn the appliqués right side out. Use a turning tool to smooth the curves and push out the points. Finger-press the fabric slightly over the interfacing side so that the interfacing won't show on the finished quilt. Use an iron to press each shape from the interfacing side.

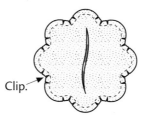 

Clip.

5. Pin a flower center to each rose and appliqué it in place. Appliqué a medium flower to each large flower, and then appliqué a flower base to each medium flower.

6. Refer to "Cutting Bias Strips" on page 7 to cut 1¼"-wide bias strips and 1"-wide bias strips from the green print. Cut the 1¼"-wide strips into 16 stems, 11" long, and 16 stems, 8½" long. Cut the 1"-wide strips, into 16 vines, 14" long. Fold each piece in half lengthwise, wrong sides together. Sew ⅛" from the raw edges of each piece. With the seam centered on the underside, press each piece flat.

MAKING THE APPLIQUÉ BLOCKS

1. Fold a light 20½" square in half and finger-press the fold. Fold in half again and finger-press the fold. Fold a B appliqué in the same manner to locate its center. Insert a pin through the center of the appliqué and then through the center of the light square. Rotate the appliqué to align the creased lines and pin the appliqué in place.

2. Pin a rose unit in each corner of a light square, approximately 1¼" from the outer edges. Curve an 8½" stem from one corner of the center appliqué to the rose, tucking the ends under the appliqués. Pin the stem in place. Make a mark 9¼" from one corner of the light square. Tucking the end under the center appliqué, curve an 11" stem from the same corner of the center appliqué to the mark. The long stem will extend beyond the edges of the block.

   Using a water-soluble marker, mark 4" from the edge of the center appliqué. You may want to draw a circle to use as a guide. Tuck one end of a 14"-long vine under the center appliqué, and then curve it into a spiral, pinning as you go. Fold under the end of the vine. Pin two leaf

appliqués to the 8½" stem and one leaf to the 11" stem.

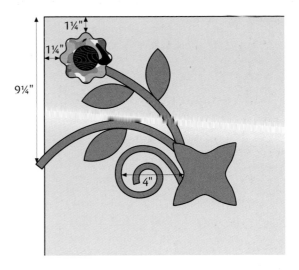

3. Repeat step 2 for the other three corners of the light square. Appliqué the pieces in place. When appliquéing the 11" stem, stop stitching about 1" from the outer edge of the light square and leave the remainder of the stem unattached. Make four appliqué blocks.

ASSEMBLING THE QUILT TOP

1. Sew two Chain blocks, one appliqué block, and two multicolored 12½" x 20½" rectangles together as shown. Pin the loose stems on the appliqué blocks out of the way so they don't get sewn into the seam allowance. Press the seam allowances away from the Chain blocks. Make two rows.

Make 2.

2. On each row from step 1, pin a large flower unit to the Chain blocks as shown, tucking the stem underneath the flower unit. Pin another leaf to the 11" stem. Appliqué the pieces in place.

3. Sew together two appliqué blocks, one Chain block, and two border units. Press the seam allowances toward the appliqué blocks. Appliqué large flowers and leaves to the 11" stems in the same manner as before. Make one of these rows.

Make 1.

4. Sew multicolored 12½" x 32½" rectangles to opposite sides of a border unit. Press the seam allowance toward the rectangles. Make two of these rows.

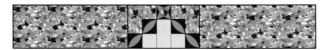

Make 2.

5. Sew a row from step 2 to each side of the row from step 3. Appliqué the large flowers and leaves in place in the same manner as before. Add the rows from step 4 to the top and bottom edges, and then appliqué the remaining large flowers and leaves in place. Refer to the photo on page 58 as needed for placement guidance.

FINISHING THE QUILT

Refer to "Finishing Techniques" on page 7 for detailed instructions.

1. Layer the quilt top, batting, and backing; baste the layers together.

2. Machine quilt in the ditch along the outer edges of the purple squares. Free-motion quilt around the curved edges of the pink appliqués; then quilt inside the pink appliqués as shown in the quilting diagram for unit A. Free-motion quilt around the flowers, leaves, vines, and flower centers. In the outer corners of the Chain blocks, use a water-soluble marker to draw a 2" grid on the background and quilt on the lines; then micro-stipple in the alternate squares. Stipple quilt the background areas. Quilt large swirls and spirals in the border.

3. Bind the quilt with the multicolored 3"-wide strips.

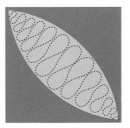

Unit A quilting diagram

Block and border quilting diagram

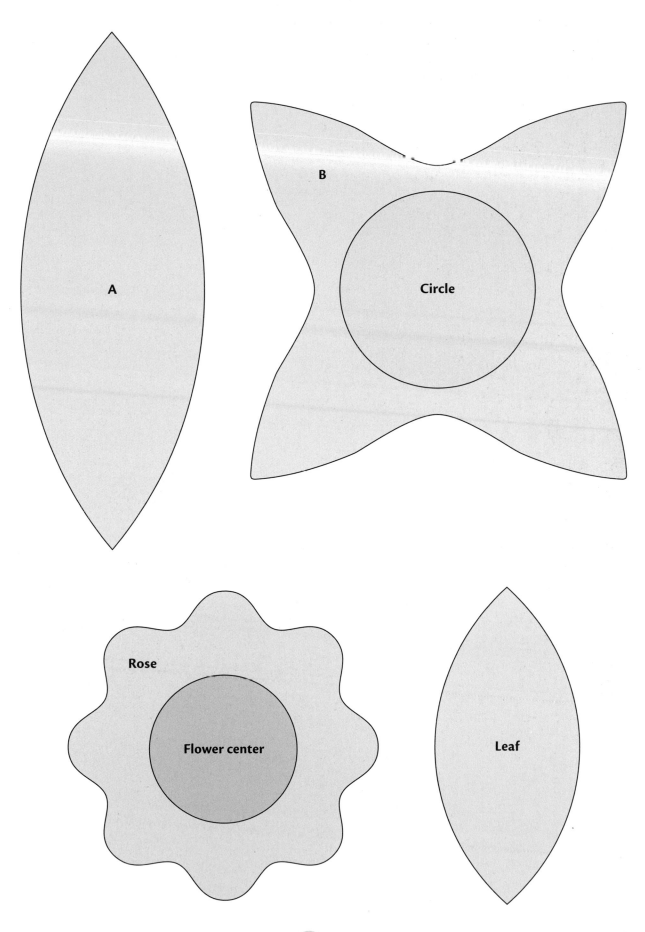

A

B

Circle

Rose

Flower center

Leaf

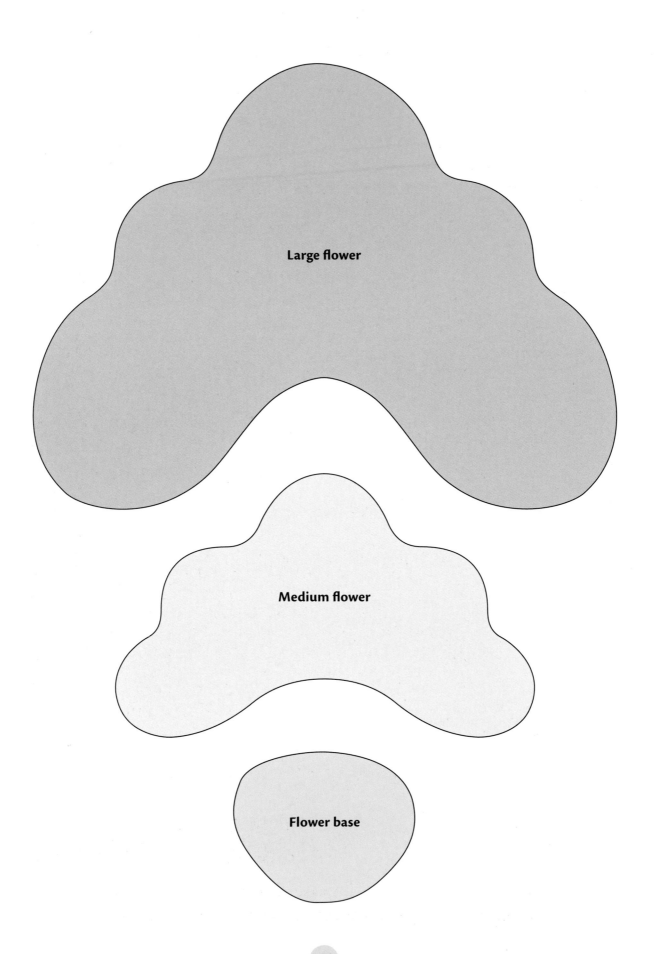

Large flower

Medium flower

Flower base

Dot to Dot

Finished quilt: 40¼" x 50"
Finished block: 7" x 7"

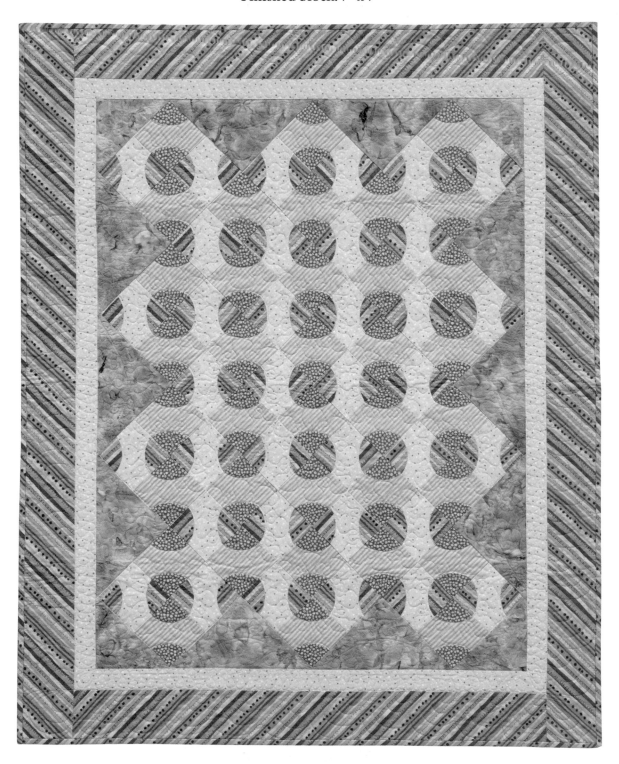

This Drunkard's Path variation is easy when you use the interfacing
appliqué technique rather than traditional curved piecing.

MATERIALS

Yardages are based on 42"-wide fabric.

1½ yards of multicolored diagonally striped fabric for blocks, outer border, and binding

¾ yard of yellow print for blocks and inner border

½ yard of green striped fabric for blocks

½ yard of brown print for blocks

½ yard of green batik for setting triangles

2½ yards of fabric for backing

44" x 54" piece of batting

¾ yard of 45"-wide lightweight non-fusible interfacing*

Template plastic

*If you use 22"-wide interfacing, you'll need 1½ yards.

CUTTING

All measurements include ¼"-wide seam allowances. Cut all strips across the width of the fabric.

From the interfacing, cut:
• 5 strips, 5" x 45"

From the multicolored diagonally striped fabric, cut:
• 3 strips, 5" x 42"
• 5 strips, 4" x 42"
• 5 strips, 3" x 42"

From the brown print, cut:
• 3 strips, 5" x 42"

From the yellow print, cut:
• 4 strips, 4" x 42"; crosscut into 36 squares, 4" x 4"
• 4 strips, 2" x 42"

From the green striped fabric, cut:
• 4 strips, 4" x 42"; crosscut into 36 squares, 4" x 4"

From the green batik, cut:
• 3 squares, 11¼" x 11¼"; cut into quarters to yield 12 side triangles (2 are extra)
• 2 squares, 6" x 6"; cut in half diagonally to yield 4 corner triangles

MAKING THE BLOCKS

Refer to "The Interfacing Technique" on page 4 for detailed instructions.

1. Make a plastic template of the circle pattern on page 70. Use the template to trace 36 circles onto the interfacing strips. Leave approximately ½" of space between shapes. Separate the strips into two sets of 18 circles each.

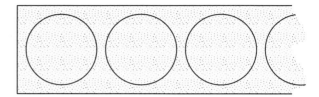

2. With right sides up, pin 18 traced circles to the multicolored 5"-wide strips. Sew on the marked lines, slightly overlapping the stitching at the beginning and end of each seam.

3. Cut out the circles, leaving ⅛" to ¼" for seam allowance. Cut a slit in the interfacing and turn the circles right side out. Smooth out the curves and finger-press the fabric slightly over the interfacing side so that the interfacing won't show on the finished quilt. Use an iron to press each circle from the interfacing side.

4. Repeat steps 2 and 3 using the brown 5"-wide strips to make 18 circle appliqués.

5. To find the midpoint on each circle, use two rulers to measure 2" from opposite sides of an appliqué circle as shown. Remove one ruler and cut the appliqué circle in half. In the same manner, cut each semicircle in half to make quarter circles.

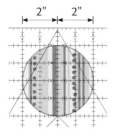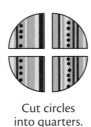

Cut circles into quarters.

6. Pin two brown quarter circles to opposite corners of each green striped square. Pin two multicolored quarter circles to opposite corners of each yellow square. Appliqué the curved edges of the quarter circles to the squares using a blanket stitch, blind hem stitch, or narrow zigzag stitch. Make 36 of each.

Make 36.   Make 36.

7. On the wrong side of each square, trim away the fabric and interfacing under each quarter-circle portion, leaving ⅛" to ¼" for seam allowance and being careful not to cut into the top fabric.

8. Arrange two yellow squares and two green striped squares in two rows of two squares each, as shown. Join the squares in each row. Press the seam allowances toward the green striped square. Join the rows and press the seam allowances to one side. Make 18 blocks.

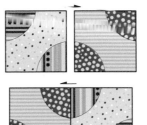

Make 18.

ASSEMBLING THE QUILT TOP

1. Lay out the blocks, green side triangles, and green corner triangles in diagonal rows as shown. Join the pieces in each row. Press the seam allowances in opposite directions from row to row. Join the rows and press the seam allowances in one direction.

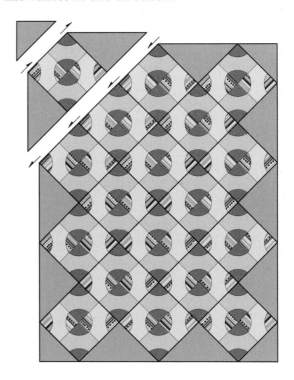

2. Refer to "Adding Borders" on page 7 to measure, cut, and sew the yellow 2"-wide strips to the sides, and then the top and bottom edges of the quilt top for the inner border. Repeat using the multicolored 4"-wide strips for the outer border.

FINISHING THE QUILT

Refer to "Finishing Techniques" on page 7 for detailed instructions.

1. Layer the quilt top, batting, and backing; baste the layers together.

2. Quilt in the ditch between all the blocks and along the borders. Free-motion quilt along the curved edges of the circle appliqués. Quilt the designs shown at right in the blocks and borders.

3. Bind the quilt using the multicolored 3"-wide strips.

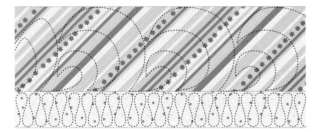

Block quilting diagram

Border quilting diagram

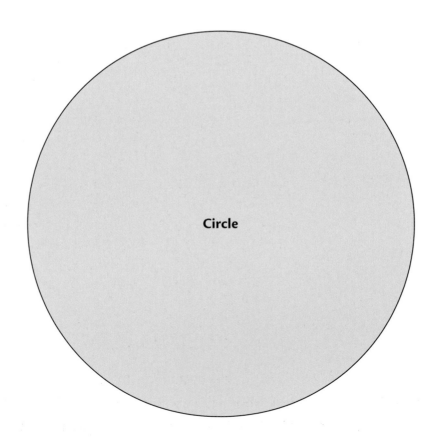

Circle

Endless Ribbon

Finished quilt: 49" x 49"

Finished block: 7½" x 7½"

This is the only quilt in the book that has a quilt center made entirely
of pieced blocks. An appliqué border on this sunny quilt allows it
to be included in the fuss-free machine appliqué family.

MATERIALS

Yardages are based on 42"-wide fabric.

2¾ yards *total* of assorted plaids for blocks, border appliqué, and binding*

2 yards of yellow print for blocks and border

3 yards of fabric for backing

53" x 53" piece of batting

¾ yard of 45"-wide lightweight non-fusible interfacing**

Template plastic

Water-soluble marker

*If using fat quarters, you'll need 13 total: you can make 2 blocks, 3 border appliqués, and 1 binding strip from each fat quarter.

**If using 22"-wide interfacing, you'll need 1½ yards.

CUTTING

All measurements include ¼"-wide seam allowances. Cut all strips across the width of the fabric.

From the yellow print, cut:

• 5 strips, 3⅞" x 42"; crosscut into 50 squares, 3⅞" x 3⅞"

• 5 strips, 3½" x 42"

• 7 strips, 2" x 42"; crosscut into 125 squares, 2" x 2"

• 3 strips, 2" x 42"; crosscut into:
  24 rectangles, 2" x 3½"
  4 rectangles, 2" x 4½"

• 3 squares, 3⅜" x 3⅜"; cut into quarters diagonally to yield 12 triangles

From the assorted plaids, cut *a total of:*

• 11 strips, 3" x 22"

• 2 squares, 5½" x 5½"; cut into quarters diagonally to yield 8 triangles

• 50 squares, 3⅞" x 3⅞" (25 sets of 2 matching squares)*

• 12 squares, 3⅞" x 3⅞"; cut in half diagonally to yield 24 triangles*

• 12 squares, 3½" x 3½"*

• 100 squares, 2" x 2" (25 sets of 4 matching squares)*

From the interfacing, cut:

• 2 strips, 12" x 45"

*For each block, you'll need 2 plaid 3⅞" squares and 4 plaid 2" squares, all matching. For each side unit you'll need 2 plaid 3⅞" triangles and 1 plaid 3½" square, all matching.

MAKING THE BLOCKS

1. Refer to "Making Triangle Squares" on page 6. Use two matching plaid 3⅞" squares and two yellow 3⅞" squares to make four triangle squares. The triangle squares should measure 3½" x 3½". Make a total of 25 sets of four matching triangle squares (100 total).

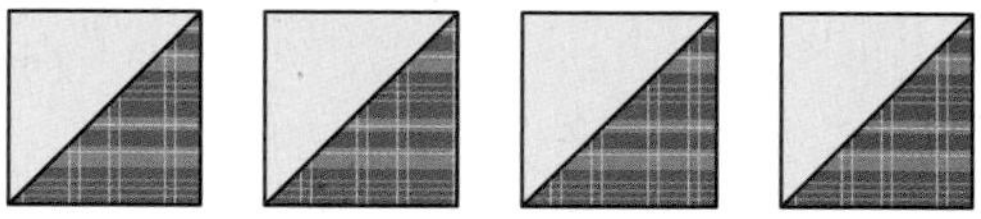

2. Sew yellow 2" squares to four matching plaid 2" squares. Make a total of 25 sets of four matching units (100 total).

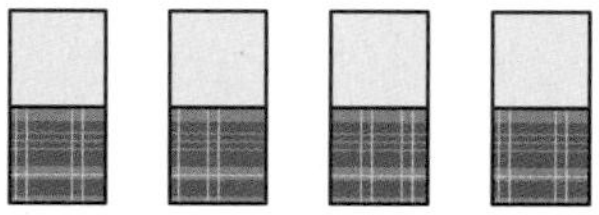

3. Using matching units, arrange four triangle squares from step 1, four units from step 2, and one yellow 2" square in three rows as shown. Join the pieces in each row. Press the seam allowances toward the plaid squares. Join the rows and press the seam allowances toward the center. Make 25 blocks.

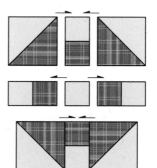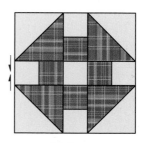

Make 25.

ASSEMBLING THE QUILT TOP

1. Arrange two matching plaid 3⅞" triangles, one matching plaid 3½" square, two yellow 2" x 3½"

rectangles, and one yellow triangle in three rows as shown. Join the pieces into rows. Press the seam allowances in opposite directions from row to row. Join the rows and press the seam allowances toward the plaid pieces. Make 12 side units.

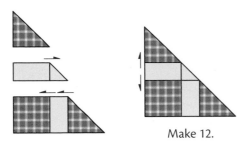

Make 12.

2. Join two matching plaid 5½" triangles to one yellow 2" x 4½" rectangle as shown. Trim the tip of the yellow rectangle even with the edges of the plaid triangles. Make four corner units.

Make 4.

3. Lay out the blocks, side units, and corner units in diagonal rows as shown. Join the blocks and units in each row. Press the seam allowances in opposite directions from row to row. Join the rows and press the seam allowances in one direction.

MAKING THE BORDER

1. Make a plastic template of the arc pattern on page 75. Use the template to trace 28 arcs onto the interfacing strips. Leave approximately ½" of space between arcs. Cut the arcs apart, leaving at least a ¼" margin of interfacing.

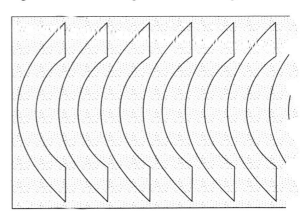

2. With right sides up, pin the marked interfacing pieces to the assorted plaids. Sew on the curved lines, leaving the short ends open. Backstitch at the beginning and end of each seam.

3. Cut out the appliqué shapes, leaving ⅛" to ¼" for seam allowance along the stitched edges and cutting directly on the straight line on each end. Clip the inner curves. Cut a slit in the interfacing and turn the appliqués right side out. Smooth out the curves and finger-press the fabric slightly over the interfacing side so that the interfacing won't show on the finished quilt. Use an iron to press each shape from the interfacing side.

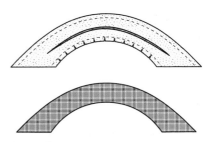

4. With right sides facing down, pin seven appliqués along each side of the quilt center, aligning the straight ends of the arcs with the edge of the quilt top. Start in one corner and work in a clockwise direction around the outer edge,

placing one end of each appliqué underneath the previous appliqué as shown.

5. Refer to "Adding Borders" on page 7 to measure, cut, and sew the yellow 3½"-wide strips to the sides, and then the top and bottom edges of the quilt top for the outer border. You'll be securing the appliqués in the seam as the borders are added. Press the seam allowances toward the quilt center.

6. Position the appliqués on top of the yellow border and press. Pin the appliqués as needed so they lie flat on the border. Appliqué the pieces in place using a blanket stitch, blind hem stitch, or narrow zigzag stitch.

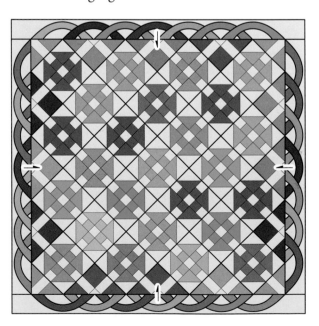

FINISHING THE QUILT

Refer to "Finishing Techniques" on page 7 for detailed instructions.

1. Layer the quilt top, batting, and backing; baste the layers together.

2. Quilt in the ditch along the yellow ribbons crisscrossing the quilt and along the seam line for the border. Free-motion quilt zigzags through the yellow ribbons. Quilt scallops in the plaid squares and triangles in each block. Using a water-soluble marker, draw a 2" circle in the center of each large yellow square. Quilt a spiral in the center and feather loops around the outside of the circle as shown in the quilting diagram. In the border, quilt along the curved edges of the appliqués; then quilt loops in each appliqué shape and stipple quilt the background.

3. Bind the quilt using the plaid 3"-wide strips.

Quilt center quilting diagram

Border quilting diagram

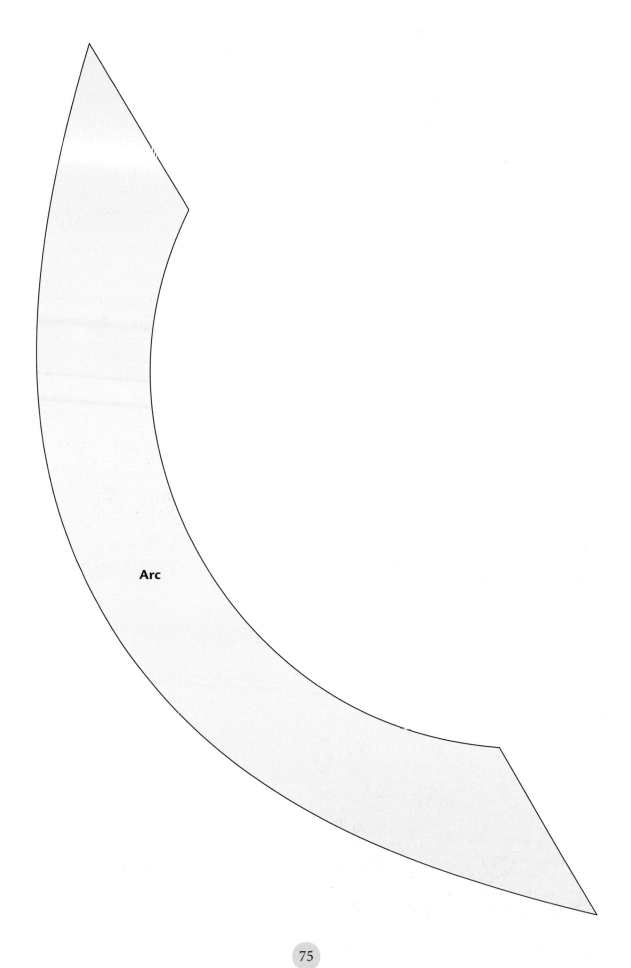

Arc

Lime Rickey

Finished quilt: 30½" x 30½"
Finished block: 12" x 12"

A zing of lime accents this cute quilt made in graphic black-and-white prints.
The addition of rickrack around the blocks is a fun accent. The Lime Rickey,
a popular cocktail in the early twentieth century, is now often made
without alcohol. The name is perfect for this happy quilt.

MATERIALS

Yardages are based on 42"-wide fabric

⅞ yard of white-with-black print for block backgrounds

½ yard of black-and-white striped fabric for block corners

¼ yard of black-with-white dotted fabric for border

½ yard of lime green print for flower-center appliqués and binding

⅜ yard of black-with-white print for flower appliqués

1 yard of fabric for backing

35" x 35" piece of batting

7 yards of bright green ¼"-wide rickrack

⅜ yard of 45"-wide lightweight non-fusible interfacing*

Template plastic

If using 22"-wide interfacing, you'll need ¾ yard.

CUTTING

All measurements include ¼"-wide seam allowance. Cut all strips across the width of the fabric.

From the white-with-black print, cut:
- 2 strips, 12½" x 42"; crosscut into 4 squares, 12½" x 12½"

From the black-and-white striped fabric, cut:
- 3 strips, 5½" x 42"; crosscut into 16 squares, 5½" x 5½"

From the black-with-white print, cut:
- 2 strips, 5" x 42"

From the lime green print, cut:
- 1 strip, 2½" x 42"
- 4 strips, 3" x 42"

From the interfacing, cut:
- 2 strips, 5" x 45"

From the black-with-white dotted fabric, cut:
- 4 strips, 3½" x 42"

From the rickrack, cut:
- 16 pieces, 9" long

MAKING THE BLOCKS

1. On the wrong side of each black-and-white striped square, draw a diagonal line from corner to corner, making sure to draw the line in the same direction across the stripes on each square.

2. With right sides together, place a marked square on each corner of a white-with-black 12½" square. The stripes should be facing in the same direction on opposite corners as shown. Sew on the marked line. Before trimming, press the resulting triangle open so that it lines up perfectly with the edges of the underlying square. Fold back the top triangle and trim away both corner triangles, leaving a ¼" seam allowance. Make four blocks, making sure the striped squares are in the same position on each block.

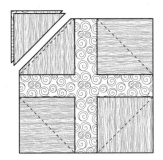

Make 4.

3. Make a plastic template of the flower and circle shapes using the patterns on page 79. Refer to "The Interfacing Technique" on page 4 as needed.

4. Use the flower template to trace 16 shapes onto the 5"-wide interfacing strips. Leave approximately ½" of space between shapes. Use the circle template to trace four shapes onto the remaining interfacing strips in the same manner. Cut the traced flower centers from the strips, leaving the flowers joined in strips.

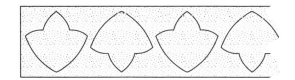

5. With right sides up, pin each flower interfacing strip to a black-with-white 5"-wide strip and the circle interfacing shapes to the lime green 2½"-wide strip. Sew on the marked lines of each shape, slightly overlapping the stitches at the beginning and end of each seam.

6. Cut out the appliqué shapes, leaving ⅛" to ¼" for seam allowance. Clip the inner points of the flower shapes. Cut a slit in the interfacing of each shape and turn the appliqués right side out. Use a turning tool to smooth the curves and push out the points. Finger-press the fabric slightly over the interfacing side so that the interfacing won't show on the finished quilt. Use an iron to press each shape from the interfacing side.

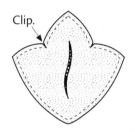

Clip.

7. Pin four flowers in the center of each block, leaving a small space between each flower. Pin a circle in the center of the block, covering the base of each flower. Appliqué the shapes in place using a blanket stitch, blind hem stitch, or small zigzag stitch. Make four appliquéd blocks.

Make 4.

8. Place a 9" rickrack piece on top of the seam line for the corner triangles, as shown. Stitch the rickrack in place using a thread color that matches the rickrack.

ASSEMBLING THE QUILT TOP

1. Arrange and sew the blocks into two rows of two blocks each. Press the seam allowances in opposite directions from row to row. Sew the rows together and press the seam allowances in one direction.

2. Refer to "Adding Borders" on page 7 to measure, cut, and sew the black-with-white dotted 3½"-wide strips to the sides, and then the top and bottom edges of the quilt top for the outer border.

3. Starting in one corner and using a thread color that matches the rickrack, sew the remaining rickrack over the seam line between the quilt center and the border, pivoting at the corners. As your approach the last corner, stop sewing with the needle in the down position. Determine how much rickrack you'll need to finish the seam, trim the rickrack ¼" beyond what is needed, and turn under the cut end ¼". Continue sewing the rickrack down and backstitch.

FINISHING THE QUILT

Refer to "Finishing Techniques" on page 7 for detailed instructions.

1. Layer the quilt top, batting, and backing; baste the layers together.

2. Machine quilt on top of the rickrack; then free-motion quilt in the ditch around the flower petals and flower centers. Quilt the design shown below in the flower appliqués. Stipple quilt the block background and zigzag quilt in the striped triangles following the direction of the stripes. Quilt a continuous design in the outer border.

3. Bind the quilt using the lime green 3"-wide strips.

Quilting diagram

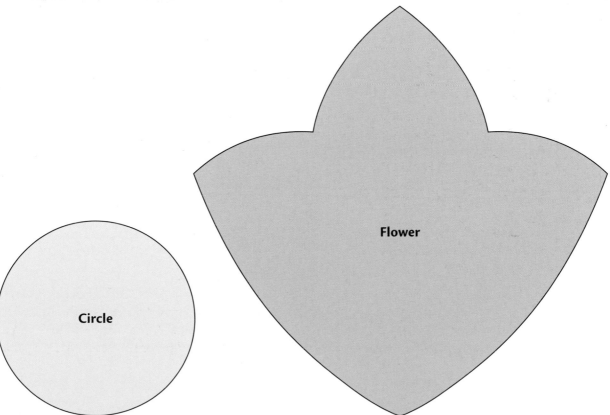

Circle

Flower

Acknowledgments

As always, thanks to my quilting communities, The Cal-Co Quilters' Guild and the Ladies of the Lake, who provide me with inspiration and feedback, and to Doris Kaiser who is my sounding board and quilting companion. My thanks to the Martingale & Company family who have taken my quilts and shown them so beautifully and taken my thoughts and ideas and brought them to life.

About the Author

Designer Lori Buhler has been quilting for more than 20 years. She learned to stitch many types of needlework as a child, but once she discovered quilting in the 1980s, she became hooked and hasn't looked back since. Although she began making quilts using traditional hand-sewing methods, she has learned to appreciate the faster results of machine work.

Lori enjoys sharing quilting with others and believes that her designs should be just a starting place for each quilter to develop her own unique quilts. She is especially interested in helping today's busy quilters find easier ways to achieve a more complicated look. In addition to being an active member of several quilting groups, she has also won numerous regional awards, including Quilter of the Year from the Cal-Co Quilters' Guild in 2001. Lori's first book, *Quilter's Happy Hour,* was also published by Martingale & Company (2008). Lori lives with her family in Battle Creek, Michigan.

There's More Online!
Visit martingale-pub.com to find great quilting and sewing books, ebooks, free patterns, and more.